Ukrainian Soul

Ukrainian Soul

The Story of the Family *Volkoff* from Borzna

With Memoirs of Joe DuVal (Volkoff) Growing up in Wisconsin
Early 20th century through 1958

David S. DuVal

iUniverse, Inc.
New York Lincoln Shanghai

Ukrainian Soul
The Story of the Family Volkoff from Borzna

iUniverse, Inc.

For information address:
iUniverse, Inc.
2021 Pine Lake Road, Suite 100
Lincoln, NE 68512
www.iuniverse.com

ISBN: 0-595-31967-X (Pbk)
ISBN: 0-595-66450-4 (Cloth)

Printed in the United States of America

Volkoff Family—1906

(r-l: Peysach, Marion, Sally, Joe, Motley, Florence

CONTENTS

Preface xi

Introduction 1

Beginnings 3

Historical Background 7

Historical Roots 10

The Pale of Settlement 13

Growing up in Borzna 20

The End of the World—1899-1900 34

Decision 36

The Voyage 47

The Arrival 54

Pictures from Borzna 64

Citizenship 71

Future Work 80

My Life: An Autobiography 81

Volkovitsky Time-Line 168

Bibliography 177

PREFACE

Relatives have always confused me; not the people but the relationships. My parents never used the words "mother" or "father"; I knew them simply as "Roz" and "Joe". For many years I had no idea this was unusual. As for the familial labels for relatives beyond my immediate family, they were complete mysteries. The word "aunt" was simply the first name of an "Aunt Fanny" who was somehow related to me. (I discovered much later that she was actually a great-aunt, and that what I thought was her last name, Fanny, turned out to be her first name!) Although we had occasional visits with relatives, I had no idea of what was inherent in the concepts of aunt, uncle, nephew, niece, or cousin. When these became prefaced by "great" or appended with "once-removed", it was like explaining trigonometry to someone who was just learning to write numbers and didn't really know yet why numbers were important to know.

This began to change several years ago while helping my wife, Ruth, pursue her family history. I've always enjoyed research, and it was intriguing to uncover information that kept extending my acquaintance with her family further back in time. She eventually compiled this research into a book, copies of which were shared with other family members. Much of this information was becoming increasingly difficult to accumulate. Eventually, it would have become lost to future generations.

I became convinced that I needed to do something similar. Both my mother and father had passed away, but each left a wealth of historical material which included photographs, scrapbooks, and even autobiographies. As I began to peruse this material, I felt somehow responsible for it. To let it lie dormant, perhaps to be discarded, seemed almost criminal. And so I committed myself to reach back as far as I could, compile as much as possible, and set it down in a form that could be shared with all present and future family members so that they, too, could "recall".

One gentleman, answering the question "Why do we do all this?" wrote in an e-mail:

> Last week, I went to Netanya to meet with a ninety-some year old Pickholz from Skalat. Most of her family was killed in the Holocaust and neither she nor her brother had children. After about an hour of

going through the names of her many cousins, she said "So why are you doing this? Can you bring them back?"

I had no answer then, but afterwards I realized what I should have said.

No, Miriam, I cannot bring them back, but I can help to see that they do not die again when you do. Miriam, now you are no longer the only person who knows their names, and we will record them so that it will always be known that they existed.[1]

Simone Weil is quoted as saying, "To be rooted is perhaps the most important and least recognized need of the human soul. To be able to give, one has to possess; and we possess no other life, no other living sap, than the treasures stored up from the past and digested, assimilated, and created afresh by us."

100 years after this family came to America makes an appropriate date for the publication of this document. It's not the end—only a beginning—a remembrance of an event and its grand promise.

Nobel Prize winner Elie Wiesel wrote:

To remember is to create links between past and present, between past and future. To remember is to affirm man's faith in humanity and to convey meaning to our endeavors.

July 2004   David DuVal

---

[1] Israel Pickens, <u>Why do we do all this</u>, e-mail, 1 Aug 1999.

INTRODUCTION

COLLECTING THE PIECES

Ruth and I enjoy working on jigsaw puzzles. One of my jobs is to fit together all the edges. Then we fill in the puzzle itself. The fascination of this game is taking pieces that don't seem to relate and to watch as they individually form the overall scene. Finding family information and weaving it together to see what sort of picture evolves is like this activity of putting together a puzzle. The difference is that there is eventually an end to the jigsaw puzzle. There is no end, however, to <u>this</u>, our family puzzle. It actually grows as questions are asked and more information (more pieces) are fitted in.

Working on this puzzle, I have found three types of puzzle pieces. The most common is the basic information piece; the type that one normally finds making up a family tree. It contains the names of family members usually with their dates of birth and death. Since it is composed mostly of vital statistics, it is often labeled "tombstone data". It is easy to recognize, and it comprises the physical limits of the puzzle.

It is a tragedy that many families are missing even this simple information. It is also unfortunate that even though they may have this kind of information, this is all they know of their history. A person's life, unique, and dependent on what one does with it, is related directly to the LIVES of those who preceded him or her. The remembrance and appreciation of the lives of those who went before, of what they endured, of what they suffered, and of how they triumphed, gives us a sense of how we ourselves fit into this continuing drama; as Shakespeare wrote, "All the world's a stage and all the men and women merely players." Other animals use tools and even have primitive language systems, but no other creature can look at, appreciate, and, yes, love the accomplishments of previous generations, even pondering one's own place in this scheme. This is one of those activities that makes us distinctly human and gives us a chance to be what God made us to be. So even if all we have is "tombstone data", it is worthy of being preserved and passed along. It spurs our imagination and provides the grist for further exploration and discovery.

A second type of puzzle piece provides what can be called "historical perspective". This includes vocations, geographical movements, historical and cultural environments. For example, when, how, and why did the person immigrate to America? What were the conditions that caused it, and what were the challenges faced? It is with the answers to these questions (or perhaps it is with simply asking the questions) that the 'family tree' ceases to be a simple two-dimensional diagram. The names take on the personae of real people, and the events which affected them become part of our lives as well. Their history lives within each of us as their descendants. It is the soil in which stretch the roots of our tree. Compared with the first puzzle piece type, this variety is more difficult to find, especially as one goes farther back in time. Still, much can be gained with the artifacts that have been left, as well as that which can be gleaned from civil records, library research, and even diaries of others who were their contemporaries.

The third piece is the one that is early lost and extremely difficult to recover, because it is rarely recorded. It tells us who a person really was. It gives us their personality, their likes and dislikes. This piece is the puzzle's soul and is that which brings us closer to those who came before us—even when this piece represents pure speculation. Diaries, letters, even oral stories that have passed down are rare gems. Wouldn't we love to have some of these from our grandparents.

The family tree is reminiscent of the shopping mall map with its small red arrow labeled: "YOU ARE HERE!" It simply tells us where we are; the other pieces tell us why we're here, and how we came to be here.

Finally, so what? Is this really important? Why should we care? What difference does it make? A Jewish proverb states, "*If you save the life of one person, it is as if you saved the world entire.*" Grace Paley in her book, *Debts*, wrote:

> (It is hard) to have family archives or even stories about grandparents or uncles when one is sixty or seventy and there was no writer in the family and the children were in the middle of their own lives. It is a pity to lose this inheritance just because of one's own family and the families of my friends. That is, to tell their stories…in order, you might say, to save a few lives.[2]

So, now I shall try to "save a few lives"; to set down not just a family tree, but to create a sense of the rich heritage of our family, a heritage which we can look back on with pride, which can enrich our present, and to which we can and do continue to contribute.

---

[2] Grace Paley, *Enormous Changes at the Last Minute; Stories,* Debts.

BEGINNINGS

Where does one begin? Does one start with the oldest records extant? That, of course, will always leave one feeling somewhat incomplete; there will always be that previous generation about which nothing is known. In addition, the religious person would want to go all the way back to Adam and Eve. The paleontologist wouldn't even be satisfied unless he could find the first amoeba!

Practically speaking, the mathematical possibilities quickly become ponderous. For example, let's consider only our direct relatives. That is, don't consider aunts and uncles; simply think only of parents, grandparents, etc. Each of us has two parents, four grandparents, eight great-grandparents, sixteen great-great grandparents, etc.

1	2
2	4
3	8
4	16
5	32
6	64
7	128
8	256
9	512
10	**1,024**
15	32,768
20	1,048,576
25	33,554,432
30	1,073,741,824
40	1,099,511,627,776
50	1,125,899,906,842,624

Figure 1

Figure 1 shows that after only ten generations, we have 1,024 *direct* ancestors. After twenty generations, we have over one million direct-line ancestors. Incredibly, each one had to have survived long enough to have at least one child. Each persevered through war and crime, disease and accident! This is even more impressive considering our Jewish heritage with its own special persecutions, its pogroms and its Holocaust. How special each one of us is.

The question still remains, "Where do I start?" A family tree with over a thousand direct relatives (not to mention all the brothers and sisters, aunts and uncles and cousins) is impossible to imagine—perhaps we are fortunate most of us can look back only a few generations.

Some have written tongue-in-cheek accounts that take a tree back to biblical times. For example:

> In a message dated 5/26/99 10:44:59 PM Eastern Daylight Time, snoopy writes:
>
> << Searched an ancient document and found I had an ancestor named JAPHETH. He had two brothers, SHEM and HAM. Their dad was involved in shipbuilding in some sort of worldwide capacity and later branched out into vineyards and winemaking. If any of this sounds familiar, email me. We could be cousins. >>
>
> I think we may well be related. As far as I know, I'm descended from his son Shem. The father was a multifaceted person: in addition to the shipbuilding business he was deeply involved in ecology—zoological preservation and flood control were among his passions; he was also a pigeon fancier. According to family tradition, he was very much a loner and rarely mingled with anyone outside his immediate family, but he did set up a trust to redeem alcoholics. He was, apparently, a real "survivor" as we'd say today. I've been trying to get the shipping records but I run into a real mountain as I check out where he may have landed. Anyone else related to this family?[3]

---

[3] Michael Benet, <u>Searched ancient document and found ancestor</u>, e-mail, May 1999, New York.

And this:

> I am so excited! We've always thought that our family should be "numerous like the stars in the sky" (BTW, does that ring a bell?)—
>
> Family lore has it that we, too, have an ancestor who, in fact, built the biggest ship of his time, and he was into wine growing as well. I'm not sure about the spelling of his name but my ggf said it sounded something like "Noach" (Noakh in English), and when the family went to live abroad later on, the guttural "ch" sound somehow got lost—Would it be rash to assume that we may be related? Do you know anything about his wife, or the wives of his sons? BTW, my gf said there's a story about a big scandal around one of them—
>
> I've had the same problem with ships' records and found an interesting piece of literature that has been on the market forever altho under various names, moreover the author(s?) apparently wanted to remain anonymous—try any bookshop for "Genesis", they should have it if they are any good. It's written in semi-documentary style so it's hard to tell what's "hard facts"…There's a possibility that back then, they did not keep records, or at least not systematically. But I've heard that a number of scholars and researchers have worked on it for quite a while, there even used to be some sort of "school" somewhere over in the Middle East, if I remember right it was either Palestine or Babylonia?
>
> Other names I've found out are Aram, Ophir, Kusch and Kittim but I haven't been able to establish exactly the lines of relation. Do you have any of these names in your tree?[4]

Seriously though, for us here in America, there is a special generation—an important *beginning*. It is not so far back that it is difficult to know or document. It is the one that first came to America—the pioneers. What they did had enormous implications for us. If it were not for them and what they did, we might

---

[4] Maimouni, Miriam, <u>Found ancestor in ancient document</u>, e-mail, Berlin, Germany.

today be living in a Ukrainian *schtetl*, experiencing the birth pangs of a demo-cratic movement struggling against the might of a history of oppression. We might not even have been born, our ancestors having perished with so many oth-ers in a pogrom, or in the Nazi Holocaust. And, indeed, some relatives who remained behind did perish this way.

What was it like to be an immigrant? Will we ever know what it really meant to leave mother and father, children, dear friends, and "home" to come to a strange land, where one couldn't read the signs or understand the speech, and where the future was unknown? True, many left to escape terrible persecution or poverty, to where the unknown was preferable to the known. Yet, it requires great courage and faith to leave one's family and home *forever* for an uncertain future.

For us today there are two who did: Pesach and Motley Volkovitsky. In a cer-tain sense, Pesach and Motley are our "Moses"; their emigration, our "Exodus". They are our "beginning."

HISTORICAL BACKGROUND

REMINISCENCES

How far back can we go with these pioneers? Often we must simply use our imagination, using records others have written. For us, the Volkoffs, there is no firsthand account. My father, Joe, wrote his autobiography but never mentions what experiences his father and mother may have told him. Perhaps they never said. His sisters do not remember their ever recalling life before coming to America. As we shall see, there were events occurring when they left their homeland that they wouldn't want to recall. They were trying to create a new life—to establish a new "homeland." Perhaps this requires suppressing memories, even pleasant ones. But how we would love to ask them questions now.

Fortunately, others did leave a record, and we can gain some insight with these. Jewish experiences in one *schtetl* were undoubtedly similar to life in another.

What we do know is that both Pesach and Motley lived in Borzna, a small town in Ukraine. Although my father never mentions it, his sisters recall that this was the place they came from. (This is verified by a notation on a manifest of the ship on which Pesach immigrated.) My father's memoirs begin with

> My father never played fiddle for the Czar, but he did play the clarinet
> in the Czar's army band just after the turn of the century; that is, until
> he went AWOL with the Russo-Japanese War brewing.

One of his sisters, Rosalie, remembers her mother talking about being in a sleigh in the woods that surround Borzna and being chased by wolves. She also vaguely remembers that they ran a small grain store in Borzna. This is all that has come down from these pioneers about their personal experiences in the "old country"—*di alte heym*. To go back in time will require knowledge of the history of the region…and some imagination.

One researcher, whose relative remembered that she lived about a day's journey by sleigh out of Kiev, figured that a sleigh could go about 5 MPH and that a day's journey would therefore be about 25-30 miles.[5] (Borzna is about 100 miles from Kiev, which would take that journey about four to five days.

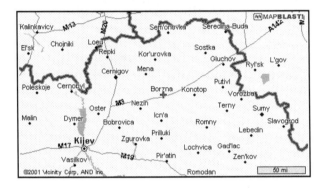

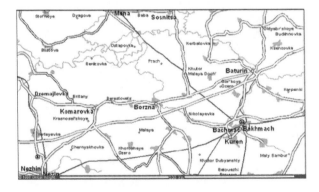

---

[5] M.P.Chijener, <u>To Kiev by horsedrawn sleigh</u>, e-mail, 2/28/2000.

Before doing that, let's take the time to find Borzna. Looking at a map, one can easily locate it in western Ukraine. First, find the capital, Kiev. Go north a few miles up the Dnieper River to where the Desna River feeds into it. The Desna comes from the north where, at a city called Chernigov, it curves east. Along this course, where the river bulges southward, is Borzna. It is located on the main road that goes from Kiev to Moscow.

For some good maps and other information on Borzna, one can find it on the internet at the following URL:

www.jewishgen.org/ShtetLinks/borzna/borzna.htm

In fact, a good deal of information about Jewish Genealogy (and more specifically about Ukraine) can be found at the JewishGen web site. Most of the e-mails used in this account are from the discussion group there and can be accessed for further information using their archives.

HISTORICAL ROOTS

Who were Pesach's parents? Motley's? Who were their grandparents? What were the events that led to the point in time of their births? When did their roots sink into the deep soil of Ukraine? Answers to these questions are speculative. Perhaps they are more interesting to dream about than actually knowing. But to do so we need to look at the history of Ukraine. Most of this history is summarized in the Timeline at the end of this essay. The following account simply fills in this synopsis.

According to some historical records, Jews were in Ukraine before the tenth century. In approximately the year 740, the King of the Khazars, along with his tribe, gave up his paganism and adopted Judaism. The Khazars were a Turkic tribe with roots in central Asia. They controlled a huge empire stretching across what is now Eastern Ukraine and Southern Russia. The Khazarian Empire survived until 965 and to a limited extent for another 50 years. Some believe that Eastern European Jews were, to a significant extent, descendents of the Khazars. Others dispute this, believing that Eastern European Jews descended from Israelite Jews who had first migrated to Southern Europe and over a millennium migrated through Europe in a generally eastern direction.[6]

In 970 many Jews fled north from the Crimea to Kiev. While William was conquering Normandy, Chaucer writing his *Tales*, and Columbus discovering the New World, the Jews were active in their own section of Kiev called *Zhydove* (pronounce zh like the z in azure), the entrance to which was known as *Zhidivski vorotan* (Jewish gate).

In 988 Prince Vladimir adopted Christianity in Kievan Rus. The year before, while he was still trying to decide between Christianity, Judaism, and Islam, Jews had attempted to convert him. How history would have changed had they been successful.

Jews continued to flow into Ukraine to Kiev during the 11th and 12th centuries, many fleeing the Crusaders, marking the appearance in Ukraine of the first western-European Jews (from Germany.) Although the Ukrainian princes were

---

[6] Estell Guzik, <u>19th Conference on Jewish Genealogy, Aug 8-13, 1999-Khazars & Europe Map</u>, e-mail, 20 Apr 1999.

supportive of their Jewish subjects, especially in the fields of trade and finance, there were periods of anti-Semitic activities including an uprising in 1133 in which the *Zhidove* district was ransacked. In fact, during the rule of Prince Monomakh, the Jews were expelled from Kiev altogether.

Whether or not there were Volkovitskys/Sovitskys there, we don't know. Exactly when "we" arrived is unknown. But the fact that we don't know gives us the right to dream of the possibility. At this time in history we do know that we had relatives somewhere. We also know that they weren't in Borzna, since at this time there was no "Borzna."

In 1264 the Polish Prince Boleslav granted the Polish Jews a charter of privileges which guaranteed their property and communities. Following Boleslav came Casimir the Great. And he truly was "great" as far as the Jews were concerned. Overlooking German bigotry and defying church opposition, he openly invited large numbers of German Jews to Poland, providing a refuge from western massacres.

> A researcher from Brown University points out that the word *pogrom* is a Russian word meaning attack and is not used as an attack on Jewish communities until the late 19th century. Up until 1881 the word used was massacre.[7]

Casimir had the foresight to see the value of a Jewish population in developing trade and commerce. His tolerance was responsible in large part to a sharp increase in the populations of several Jewish communities.

Following Casimir, between the 14th and 15th centuries, anti-Jewish restrictions became more widespread, eventually excluding Jews from conducting business in major cities. This led to a large-scale migration east into Ukraine. Could our ancestors have arrived in Ukraine at this time, driven eastward from Poland and perhaps Germany? These central European Jews (*Ashkenazim*) spoke Yiddish, wore distinctive dress, and lived apart from the local population, either in ghettos within large cities or in small, predominantly Jewish settlements (*schtetls*). They were poorer than the earlier Jewish immigrants to Ukraine. Most were engaged in petty trade since they were barred from owning land and from the professions. They were protected by the Polish monarchs (the Ukraine was then under Polish rule) and paid taxes to the king. They in turn were allowed a form of self government (Kahal) by decrees

---

[7] Judith Romney Wegner, Info on Pogroms, e-mail, 11/12/2000.

dating back to 1264. The late 15th century was also the scene of many raids by Tartars who seized many Jews to be sold into slavery in the Crimea.

The largest Jewish migration to Ukraine occurred during the late 16th century. Between 1569 and 1648 the Jewish population in Ukraine went from 4,000 to 51,300. It was during this time that Borzna was founded in 1633.

We have to hope that our relatives weren't there then, for the Ukrainian chief or Hetman, Bogdan Chmielnicki along with hundreds of Ukrainian peasants, slaughtered over 200,000 Jews during the ten year period between 1648 and the next century, wiping out over 700 Jewish communities.

Jews did not have surnames at this time. In Russia, surnames were rare for anyone but the nobility and foreign immigrants before the 19th century. Czar Alexander I (1801-25) appears to be the man who decreed that all his subjects take surnames.

The Russian czars tried to keep Jews out of their holdings as much as possible. In 1727 and again in 1739 Jews were ordered to leave Russia and what was Ukraine. Czarina Elizabeth, who ruled from 1741 to 1762, was entreated by Ukrainian merchants to be allowed to trade in Ukraine. Her reply, "From the enemies of Christ, I wish neither gain nor profit", reflected the animus against Jews, stemming from Christian beliefs that the Jews had killed Christ.

Schtetl is the diminutive of the Yiddish word for *Schtot* meaning "town". These Jewish communities began around the 15th century in Lithuania/Poland and in the Russian Pale of Settlement (see next section.) Eventually they were destroyed during the Nazi Holocaust. Most in this community were poor, working as peddlers, tailors, cobblers, or maintaining a niche within the marketplace (the locus for business as well as the main area of contact with the Gentile world.) In spite of their poverty, the inhabitants enjoyed warm and intimate times during Sabbaths and holidays Th center of the community was the synagogue with the rabbi as the center of authority. The two characteristics that marked the schtetl were *Yiddishkeit* (Jewishness) and *menshlichkeit* (humaness). As noted by one authority and as reflected within this account, "To a younger generation the schtetl seemed a cramped and arid prison from which they sought to escape." Still, reading Isaac Bashevis Singer or Sholom Aleichem revives a certain nostalgia for this genus of life, a life which was eliminated and has, for all intents and purposes, become extinct[8]

---

[8] Joan Comay. *The Diaspora story: the epic of the Jewish people among the nations*, p.212.

THE PALE OF SETTLEMENT

The Pale of Settlement was an issue at this time and during the historical period of the generation of our families. Therefore, we should know something about it and how it affected us.

Figure 2—The Pale[9]

Borzna—@ 100 miles NE of Kicv

[9] Martin Gilbert, *Jewish History Atlas*, p. vii.

Pale is the English translation of the Russian word *Cheta,* Pale being an old English term for an enclosed area, which indeed it was, for Jews could live only there within its borders. Even there, major cities within its borders, such as Kiev, Odessa and Warsaw, excluded Jews except those with special permission. All the rest of Russia was barred to Jews.

This all begins in 1791 when Czarina Catherine II sets aside a "Pale of Settlement" restricting Jewish residence to one of two areas—along Russia's western border in territories annexed from Poland, or to territories taken from the Turks along the Black Sea. Later, in an area approximately 386,000 square miles, stretching from the Baltic to the Black Sea, the Pale was created by a decree of Czar Nicholas I in April 1835. This law was finally revoked in 1917 by the Bolshevik revolution, so this area was extant almost 95 years, most of the eighteenth and the first part of the nineteenth centuries. According to the census of 1897, there were about 4,899,300 Jews within its borders. Of these most were in the urban cities, sometimes comprising a majority of the population.[10] Also, almost all of these were in Polish territory annexed by Russia during the various partitions of Poland.

> In the provinces of the Pale of Settlement, Jews form approximately one-ninth of the population. As their number increases due to the high birth rate and better medical care, the confinement to the Pale causes growing poverty. Massive expulsions from the villages, and the restrictions on professions and trade, increases competition among a growing number of people.
>
> Within the Pale, the number of artisans per 1000 persons is three times higher than elsewhere. Although the government encourages Jews to engage in agriculture, the special settlements allotted for this purpose in Southern Russia cannot absorb the tens of thousands who are driven out of the villages. During the reign of Nicholas I, the position of the Jews deteriorates significantly. To alienate them from their religion, Jews are conscripted from 1827 onward into the army for a period of no less than 25 years. The Jewish communities are made responsible

---

[10] The Jewish Student Online Research Center (JSOURCE), The Pale of Settlement, http://www.us-israel.org/jsource/History/pale.html, 2000.

for supplying a required number of recruits ("Cantonists") aged between 12 and 25. Kidnapping by so-called "khapers" is often necessary to fill the quota. The children are to be "re-educated," and compulsory instruction in Christian religion and physical pressure are used to induce them to convert. In 29 years between 30,000 and 40,000 Jewish children served as "Cantonists."

In 1843, the Jews are expelled from Kiev where they had lived for centuries. A new wave of expulsions follows when Jews are no longer allowed to live within 50 versts (1 verst = .6629 miles) of the western border. Even government officials consider the conditions in the Pale untenable. The governor of Kiev province, where 600,000 Jews live, urges the government in 1861 to lift the residence restrictions in order to relieve the congestion in the Pale.

Outside the cities, the typical Jewish community in the Pale is the shtetl (mestechko), which usually has a few thousand inhabitants and is centered around the synagogue and marketplace. Jews earn their living as petty traders, middlemen, shopkeepers, peddlers and artisans, often working with women and children as well. Those who are no longer able to find any employment join the growing number of Luftmenshen—doing anything to earn a living. At the end of the century, the Jewish population has become so impoverished that approximately one-third depend to some degree on Jewish welfare organizations. Although Jews are allowed to enter general schools, not many do because instructions are given in either Polish, Russian or German—not in Yiddish, which is by far the most widely spoken. From 1844 onward, special schools for Jews are established with the purpose of bringing them "nearer to the Christians and to uproot their harmful beliefs which are influenced by the Talmud." A special tax on candles is imposed to pay for them.

Jewish parents regard these schools with suspicion and continue to send their children to the traditional kheyder. There, the melamed (teacher) instructs the children in the Hebrew language. As the Hebrew alphabet is also used for Yiddish, the children are able to read and write in their mother tongue as well. The number of students attending the Jewish state schools is very small: about 6000 in 1864. Some enter the mainstream of the Russian intelligentsia, and in this respect the schools fulfill their purpose. A number of these students later join the protest movement against the oppressive Czarist regime.

In spite of the difficult circumstances, Jewish cultural life develops and flourishes in the Pale. From the Pale emerges a group of writers who can be considered the founding fathers of modern secular Hebrew and Yiddish literature, and many of them become world famous.[11]

An account of what life in the Pale was like is in an essay by Mary Antin called *A Little Jewish Girl in the Russian Pale, 1890*. The following is from that account.

The Gentiles used to wonder at us because we cared so much about religious things about food and Sabbath and teaching the children Hebrew. They were angry with us for our obstinacy, as they called it, and mocked us and ridiculed the most sacred things. There were wise Gentiles who understood. These were educated people, like Fedora Pavlovna, who made friends with their Jewish neighbors. They were always respectful and openly admired some of our ways. But most of the Gentiles were ignorant. There was one thing, however, the Gentiles always understood, and that was money. They would take any kind of bribe, at any time. They expected it. Peace cost so much a year, in Polotzk. If you did not keep on good terms with your Gentile neighbors, they had a hundred ways of molesting you. If you chased their pigs when they came rooting up your garden, or objected to their children maltreating your children, they might complain against you to the police, stuffing their case with false accusations and false witnesses. If you had not made friends with the police, the case might go to court; and there you lost before the trial was called unless the judge had reason to befriend you.

The cheapest way to live in Polotzk was to pay as you went along. Even a little girl understood that. In your father's parlor hung a large colored portrait of Alexander III. The czar was a cruel tyrant—oh, it was whispered when doors were locked and shutters tightly barred, at night—he was a Titus, a Haman, a sworn foe of all Jews—and yet his portrait was

---

[11] Beyond the Pale—The History of Jews in Russia,
    http://www.friends-partners.org/partners/beyond-the-pale/english/31.html

seen in a place of honor in your father's house. You knew why. It looked well when police or government officers came on business.

The czar was always sending us commands,—you shall not do this and you shall not do that,—till there was very little left that we might do, except pay tribute and die. One positive command he gave us: You shall love and honor your emperor. In every congregation a prayer must be said for the czar's health, or the chief of police would close the synagogue. On a royal birthday every house must fly a flag, or the owner would be dragged to a police station and be fined twenty-five rubles. A decrepit old woman, who lived all alone in a tumble-down shanty, supported by the charity of the neighborhood, crossed her paralyzed hands one day when flags were ordered up, and waited for her doom, because she had no flag. The vigilant policeman kicked the door open with his great boot, took the last pillow from the bed, sold it, and hoisted a flag above the rotten roof.

The czar always got his dues, no matter if it ruined a family. There was a poor locksmith who owed the czar three hundred rubles, because his brother had escaped from Russia before serving his time in the army. There was no such fine for Gentiles, only for Jews; and the whole family was liable. Now the locksmith never could have so much money, and he had no valuables to pawn. The police came and attached his household goods, everything he had, including his bride's trousseau; and the sale of the goods brought thirty-five rubles. After a year's time the police came again, looking for the balance of the czar's dues. They put their seal on everything they found...Many bitter sayings came to your ears if you were a little girl in Polotzk. "It is a false world," you heard, and you knew it was so, looking at the czar's portrait, and at the flags. "Never tell a police officer the truth," was another saying, and you knew it was good advice. That fine of three hundred rubles was a sentence of life-long slavery for the poor locksmith, unless he could free himself by some trick. As fast as he could collect a few rags and sticks, the police would be after them.

Business really did not pay, when the price of goods was so swollen by taxes that the people could not buy. The only way to make business pay was to cheat—cheat the government of part of the duties. Playing tricks on the czar was dangerous, with so many spies watching his interests. People who sold cigarettes without the government seal got more gray hairs than banknotes out of their business. The constant risk, the worry, the dread of a police raid in the night, and the ruinous fines, in case of detection, left very little margin of profit or comfort to the dealer in contraband goods. "But what can one do? "the people said, with that shrug of the shoulders that expresses the helplessness of the Pale. "What can one do? One must live."

It was not so easy to live, with such bitter competition as the congestion of population made inevitable. There were ten times as many stores as there should have been, ten times as many tailors, cobblers, barbers, tinsmiths. A Gentile, if he failed in Polotzk, could go elsewhere, where there was less competition. A Jew could make the circle of the Pale only to find the same conditions as at home. Outside the Pale he could only go to certain designated localities, on payment of prohibitive fees, which were augmented by a constant stream of bribes; and even then he lived at the mercy of the local chief of police.

Artisans had the right to reside outside the Pale on fulfillment of certain conditions which gave no real security. Merchants could buy the right of residence outside the Pale, permanent or temporary, on conditions which might at any time be changed. I used to picture an uncle of mine on his Russian travels, hurrying, hurrying, to finish his business in the limited time; while the policeman marched behind him, ticking off the days and counting up the hours. That was a foolish fancy, but some of the things that were done in Russia really were very funny.

Perhaps I should not have had so many foolish fancies if I had not been so idle. If they had let me go to school—but of course they didn't. There was one public school for boys, and one for girls, but Jewish children were admitted in limited numbers—only ten to a hundred; and even the lucky ones had their troubles. First, you had to have a tutor at home, who prepared you and talked all the time about the examination you would have to pass, till you were scared. You heard on all sides that the brightest Jewish children were turned down if the examining officers did not like the turn of their noses. You went up to be examined with the other Jewish children, your heart heavy about that matter of your nose. There was a special examination for the Jewish candidates, of course: a nine-year-old Jewish child had to answer questions that a thirteen-year-old Gentile was hardly expected to answer. But that did not matter so much; you had been prepared for the thirteen-year-old test. You found the questions quite easy. You wrote your answers triumphantly—and you received a low rating, and there was no appeal.

I used to stand in the doorway of my father's store munching an apple that did not taste good any more, and watch the pupils going home from school in twos and threes; the girls in neat brown dresses and black aprons and little stiff hats, the boys in trim uniforms with many buttons. They had ever so many books in the satchels on their backs. They would take them out at home, and read and write, and learn all sorts of interesting things. They looked to me like beings from another world than mine. But those whom I envied had their troubles, as I often heard. Their school life was one struggle against injustice from instructors, spiteful treatment from fellow students, and insults from everybody. They were rejected at the universities, where they were admitted in the ratio of three Jews to a hundred Gentiles, under the same debarring entrance conditions as at the high school: especially rigorous examinations, dishonest marking, or arbitrary rulings without disguise. No, the czar did not want us in the schools.[12]

---

[12] Eva March Tappan, ed., *The World's Story: A History of the World in Story, Song and Art, Vol. VI: Russia, Austria-Hungary, The Balkan States, and Turkey*, pp. 243-247.

GROWING UP IN BORZNA

Augustin 1878 saw the birth of Pesach Volkovitsky. Two years later in September 1880, Motley Nosavitsky was born. In August 1899, they were married. During this score of years, they grew up in Borzna. They went to school. In 1890 he was probably *Bar Mitzvah*.

Many people born in Europe in the last century or early in this one (and some born in the U.S. during that same period—see Sarah) did not know their exact dates of birth, and their children may not have known even what they knew. But it probably never mattered much to them either.

A word first about the surname. "Volk" is Slavic for "Wolf". This is also the symbol of the tribe of Benjamin. The suffix "-itch" or "-itsky" signifies "son of", so that Pesach's father was Wolf. The name could also be "Ze'ev" which is Hebrew for "Wolf".

Today, the wife's name is as important as the father's. Her name is often pronounced as Sawicz, Savicz, Savitch or Savic. One of the possible explanations is that Sava or Savel (Shavel) is a Russianization (Slavianization) of the name Saul.

Also, Russian Jews were first assigned permanent family names in 1826–but they didn't use them. The government wanted to keep track of the family so it would know who was draftable (often the first son was exempt) and who was allowed to marry (sometimes only the oldest son was allowed to marry) and who was taxed. Over the years, of course, we see that the surnames were used in different events registered by the government, e.g. births, marriages, deaths. Often the names varied for a long time before they became set.

What was it like to grow up in a Ukrainian village during the late nineteenth century? What were the forces acting on Pesach, Motley, and their parents? What must the conversations have been about America? How did the decision to emigrate come about? I could go on and on with questions for these two.

Although we can't now ask them these questions, and neither left much of a record for us, fortunately others did. There are a number of accounts of Jewish life in the Ukraine, at least one of which is set in their same time frame. And, whereas the circumstances are different, we can accept the fact that their lives were probably similar. Jewish customs, especially in towns and villages, would be similar. And sometimes we hear echoes of the few experiences that have been passed down from our grandparents. We can listen to the stories from that time and assume that Pesach and Motley could relate to them, nod their heads, and say, "Yes, our experience was a little different, but that's the way it was."

Schooling was an important factor in their lives. One researcher wrote:

When I was a young child, my father used to entertain me with a nonsense nursery rhyme he learned from his father who was born in Bazaliya, Volhynia gubernia, Ukraine in 1868:

Ucum, buchum, benziluchim,

shaila, paila, bupsi.

Unner woner, kooper doner,

revna spluter, blesh keputer,

BRESH!

I had thought that it may have been made up by my grandfather, but at a recent reunion of descendents of my father's shtetl (Felshtin; Podolia gubernia, Ukraine), someone told me that he had been told the same rhyme when he was a child.[13]

Certainly an important part of the life of Pesach was school. By 1897 there were over five million Jews living within the Russian Pale of Settlement. The general population in Borzna in 1897 was 12,000. Although they were severely restricted, it is noteworthy that in a country where the level of illiteracy (even as late as World War I) was 80 percent, almost all Jewish boys could read and write Hebrew and many could also read Russian. (Although there were many differences, this disparity in literacy between the Jewish and native peasantry was one of the sources of suspicion between the two. Even today, the Jewish community exerts a traditional positive influence toward education for the individual.) The traditional school was the *kheder* (room) in which children would begin their education as early as three.

The traditional school had boys of various ages within the same room. The teacher (*melamed*) was not generally a respected individual within the community, since he was regarded as having become a teacher by default, not having succeeded at anything else. Students usually met in a room in the teacher's home. Their books were only a prayer book, the Bible, the Talmud, and perhaps some rabbinical writings.

[13] Mel Werbach, <u>A nonsense rhyme: within the family, the shtetl or?</u> e-mail, 30 May 1999, Tarzana,California.

Here's one description from a nineteenth-century Jewish writer of a visit to a
kheder:

> Soon a poorly clad couple entered, the man carrying in his arms a young
> boy of about six, wrapped in a *talit* [prayer shawl]. Both father and
> mother were weeping with joy, grateful to God who had preserved them
> that they might witness this beautiful moment. Having extended a cordial
> welcome to the newcomers, the *melamed* [teacher] took the hero of the
> celebration into his arms and stood him upon a table. Afterwards the boy
> was seated on a bench and was the first to receive cake, nuts, raisins, and
> dainties of which the happy mother had brought along an apron-full. The
> teacher then sat down near the youngster, placed a card with a printed
> alphabet before him and, taking a long pointer, began the first lesson by
> blessing his newly-initiated pupil that he may be raised for the study of
> Torah, marriage, and good deeds.[14]

Not all schools were like this. Here is an account of a school in Vitebsk in 1894:

> Our Talmud Torahs are filthy rooms, crowded from nine in the morn-
> ing until nine in the evening with pale, starved children. These remain
> in this contaminated atmosphere for twelve hours at a time and see
> only their bent, exhausted teachers…Their [the children's] faces are
> pale and sickly, and their bodies evidently not strong. In parties of
> twenty or thirty, and at times more, they all repeat some lesson aloud
> after their instructor. He who has not listened to the almost absurd
> commentaries of the ignorant *melamed* cannot imagine how little the
> children gain from such instruction.[15]

Finally, the renowned writer Sholom Aleichem leaves us this wonderful
account in his story *Robbers!*.

> Mazepa is our *rebbe*. His name is really Boruch Moshe, but since he's
> come down recently from Mazepevka, the town calls him the
> Mazepevker, and we kheder boys have shortened it and turned it into
> Mazepa—"dark and ugly." Generally when students crown their rebbe
> with a lovely name like that, he has earned it. Let me present him to you.

> Short, shriveled and skinny—a creep. Without a trace of a beard, mus-
> tache, or eyebrows. Not, God forbid, because he shaves, but just

---

[14] Irving Howe and Kenneth Libo, *World of Our Fathers,* p.9.
[15] Ibid. p. 9.

because they don't care to grow. They talked themselves out of it. But to compensate, he has a pair of lips on him, and, oh, my! a nose! A braided loaf, a horn, a *shofar*! And a voice like a bell, a lion's roar. How did a creature like him get such a terrifying voice? And where did he get his strength? When he grabs your arm with his skinny, cold fingers, you can see the world to come. And when he slaps you, you feel it for the next three days. He hates lengthy discussions. For the least thing, guilty or not guilty, he has one law: Lie down!

"Rebbe! Yossel Yankev Yossel's hit me."

"Lie down!"

"Rebbe!, it's a lie! He kicked me in the side first."

"Lie down!"

"Rebbe! Chaim Berl Lappes stuck his tongue out at me."

"Lie down!"

"Rebbe, lies and false hood! It was just the opposite. He gave me the high sign."

"Lie down!"

And you have to lie down. Nothing helps. Even redheaded Eli, who is already *Bar Mitzvah* and betrothed and wears a silver pocketwatch—you think he isn't beaten? Oh my, isn't he! Eli says that he'll regret those beatings. He says he'll pay Mazepa back with interest; he says he'll give him something to remember him by until he has grandchildren. That's what Eli always says after a whipping, and we answer:

"Amen. Hope so. From your mouth to God's ears."[16]

An interesting item of note is given by a Polish woman: "In Europe, when a boy reached the age of three, his father wrapped a *tallis* [prayer shawl] around him and carried him to the *kheder* for the first time. A man was given his own prayer shawl when he got married."

---

[16] Sholom Aleichem, Robbers! (3), 85-86.

Although Pesach must have attended *kheder*, he may have also attended the secular school. Here is an account of an experience of a Jewish girl in eastern Poland of attending a school in a small village:

> At the age of six, I started elementary school in the first grade. The school day began with a religious prayer, and the other children crossed themselves. I felt uncomfortable, and some of my classmates teased me, saying that I would have to cross myself too. That upset me very much; I was the only Jewish student in the school.

> The second problem was that we had six days of school. My family and I were orthodox Jews, but this did not excuse me from going to school on the Sabbath. I attended the classes on those days but didn't write. I enjoyed school and received awards for excellent schoolwork.[17]

> Saturdays after the big noon meal, Father used to teach me to read Hebrew. There was no library in the village, therefore books weren't easily available. If I read a Polish book on Saturday, which my friend lent me from her own library, Father would say, "On Sabbath you don't read Polish books, on the Sabbath you read Hebrew." He was only interested that I should know enough Hebrew to read the prayer book on the High Holidays.[18]

Another very descriptive picture of a *Kheder* is given in a book called simply *The Shtetl Book*.

> The inside of my *Kheder* consisted of a large square room divided in two by a screen. Behind the screen was the teacher's bedroom and kitchen. We used to call it "the teacher's alcove."...At the west wall, between the opening to the kitchen and the hall stood a wooden alcove. It was a sort of pantry. We always watched the *melamed's* wife open and close it and almost every school boy knew every piece of kitchenware she owned.... Near the north wall stood a long wooden bench. During the winter children would draw figures on it or play *iks-miks-driks* [tic-tac-toe]. The teacher would sit on a little pillow on his bench, near the table. At the other end was a helper [*belfer*] who taught another group of children.... The *kheder* was as noisy as a fair, especially during the winter. The children ran around from one place to

---

[17] Flueck, Toby Knobel, *Memories of my life in a Polish village, 1930-1949*, Alfred A. Knopf: Distributed by Random House, New York, 1990, p. 13.

[18] Ibid., p.26.

another; some would sit on the ground, clap their hands and sing. Others just yelled or fought with each other and made a racket. Near the teacher on the bench there would always be a new kid, brought to school for the first day and crying bitterly. The commotion was made greater by the slamming of the door. The bedlam was particularly great when a beggar would come in. (The *kheder* also served as a sort of lodging-house for wandering beggars.) The youngsters would surround him, help him unpack his bundle. From amidst the uproar one could hear several children's voices, repeating in a sweet, sorrowful chant their reading lessons or the Bible. You can imagine what went on when you consider that there were 70 or 80 children in such a *kheder*.[19]

LEARNING TO READ

From the first day on which the *belfer* showed me the letters of the *alef-beys* set out in rows, I saw leaping forth measured ranks of soldiers…When I went up again, the *belfer* showed me the form of an *alef* and asked me:

"Can you see the yoke and pair of pails?"

"That's true, upon my soul; a pair of pails!"

"Well, that's an *alef*," testified the *belfer*.

"Well, that's an *alef*," I repeated after him.

And the minute I went down the *alef* flew away.[20]

YOSL-ZISL THE MELAMED

The dusk hour was usually set aside for story-telling. And on Saturday afternoons and holidays, Yosl-Zisl sat and talked with the boys as if they were his equals.

Not only did he tell them stories from the Midrash and Talmud and miraculous tales of the holy Chassidic rabbis, but he also discussed worldly matters and explained things that puzzled them.

---

[19] Diane K. Roshkies and David G. Roshkies, *The Shtetl book*, p.150.
[20] Ibid., p.151.

When the government opened a telegraph office in the railroad station of Khelm the pupils were puzzled. "Who needs a telegraph office and how does it work?"

Yosl-Zisl explained everything. "The government needs it. A telegraph office is a must for the Czar. The Russian Empire is big, very big, and the ruler is always afraid of rebellion and trouble. So, every morning he sends telegrams to all the stations:

'Is all well in your town?'

In olden times he had to send couriers, but now he gets an answer by wire in an hour:

'All's well.'

If there's rebellion, the telegraph operator answers one word:

'Trouble.' The operator is sparing with words because each word costs money."

"But, *rebe*, the capital is hundreds and hundreds of miles away. How does the telegraph carry the words?"

"Well, they stretch wires from the capital to, say, our city. When they want to send a telegram they pinch, or twist the wire in a certain manner at the capital. The wire at our end then turns in the same manner. Each twist or turn means a definite letter. How's it possible to get an immediate response from such a distance, at the other end of the wire? Well, that shouldn't surprise you. You've seen big dogs. It may be several feet from the tip of a dog's tail to his mouth. Still as soon as you twist this tail, his mouth begins to bark."

Yosl-Zisl never lacked an answer[21]

---

[21] Ibid., p.162.

There is a wonderful account of a Jewish family living in a town near Kiev. They also emigrated to America in 1904 (which is the year Pesach left.) The father left an extensive description of their life which is very useful for us in that it parallels to a great extent the Volkovitsky experience, especially in general locale and time frame. Pesach and Motley did not leave us with personal experience, but this family gives us a good picture of what might have occurred.

Their history goes back 500 years to Madrid, Spain. The Inquisition drove them to Italy, then to Vienna, Austria for 200 years, then to Poland, and then to Ukraine. Did the Volkovitskys come from Spain? Possibly. They quite probably came to Ukraine from the West, from Poland.

Easier to extrapolate are the experiences he remembers. He recalls, for instance, the marriage of his daughter and describes events leading to the births of his grandchildren. In writing about Molke—one of 6 children—he says,

> They were all married, had families of their own. Her father picked their husbands and wives for them through a matchmaker. Her sisters didn't even know their husbands until after their weddings. She must not forget that her father looked into the other families to make sure they would be suitable and comparable to her family, and who could make a better decision than her own father, through a match-maker!…She remembered when she was six years old (1868), her mother and father used to tell her that she was the prettiest of all the girls and when she grew up the *shadchen* (matchmaker or marriage broker) would bring her a *chusan*.[22]

When she was 16, she met Simche who fell in love with her. It would be Simche and Molke who would eventually come to America, as did Pesach and Motley. Pesach was married to Motley in August 1899. Nicholas II had begun his reign as Czar five years earlier, and anti-Jewish riots had taken place up until 1899. It was not a comfortable time.

Whether Israel had employed a matchmaker for Molke and Simche, he doesn't say, just as we don't know whether one was employed for Pesach and Motley. But

---

[22] Michael Charnofsky, *Jewish life in the Ukraine; a family saga*, p.29.

we do know it was the accepted and regular tradition for marriage in the schtetl. Simche tells of his father's visit to the town matchmaker.

> He went to the town *shadchen*, Erib Zelig, a man only five feet tall with a wild red beard that covered most of his face. He wore a long coat that covered him from head to toe. Erib Zelig was a successful matchmaker. He had full lists of girls and boys and he knew their families, their circumstances, and how much each girl had for her dowry, and he had a history of each of their parents.[23]

Then, in 1901, Sarah was born to Pesach and Motley. Today, she is known as Sally. The date cannot be verified, but the family accepts July 4. Following that, two more girls were added to the growing family, Rebecca on September 26, 1902, and Florence on March 8, 1904, all in Borzna. Was Motley's mother there? What about Pesach? And three girls! What about a boy?

> Then Molke became pregnant with her first child. Rivke the mother-in-law took immediate control to safeguard every step Molke took. Milk she must drink fresh and right from the cow. Meals she was served without her lifting a plate. Rivke personally cooked a *yachale* (chicken and broth) for her every day. Rivke warned her not to make any attempt to do any work. All Molke did was to knit and embroider things for the baby.

> Her father-in law decided to go to the high rabbi, first to tell him about Molke's pregnancy…and second to invite him to the *bris* (circumcision) if the baby were a boy. Maybe the rabbi could help pray for a boy. As the time came closer he and Simche began planning the *bris*. First a name, Chaim, after Simche's grandfather. Then the rabbi to perform the operation. Then the midwife (who would come a" month before to take personal charge of Molke and be on hand all the time.

> Then the *shalash* or tabernacle had to be built for the feast and dancing. "If, God forbid, a girl was born, half of the arrangements would be a total waste, for you don't need nearly all those things for a girl. But

---

[23] Ibid., p.31.

after all, Rivke [the mother-in-law] said a boy and the rabbi said a boy. So everybody was sure it would be a boy."

Then the midwife came out of the room smiling. "It's a boy! It's a boy!", she repeated. Everybody's face lighted up, and with smiles and happiness they all wished each other *mazeltov*. Losing no time they started to work for the *bris*.

First Simche hung white sheets around the bed, printed by hand on paper the words *sheer hamalee*, and put them on the four sides of the bed. This meant Psalms, to guard the infant from evil.[24]

THE WATCH NIGHT

In olden days, the Watch Night was a far more solemn occasion than it is today. People kept a close watch for Lilith who was known to steal newborn children from their mothers during the first eight days after birth, and especially on the last night known as Watch Night.

On this last night Lilith reigned supreme. Like a cuckoo bird she either exchanged the child for one belonging to demons (this is how all evildoers are born into the world) or she killed him outright. For protection, mothers pasted up a sign on the wall on which was written: *Lilith and Her Band—Stay Out.* Also, *belfers* brought their students to read the "sh'ma" prayer every evening at the home of a newborn boy until he was circumcised. On the last night before *bris* candles were lit and poor Jews who were very learned recited Psalms and studied all night. A special dinner was made for them and charity was given out.[25]

…big meals—music—dancing—people from many towns—vodka—wine. When the fourth child was born—a girl—Simche made a party for the family only—no music, no rabbis, no *shalash*, nor anything else outside of a family gathering with a family dinner. "It wasn't because there was no money to spend and it wasn't because they didn't love the little girl. It was just that you don't do that for a girl. It is not required."

---

[24] Ibid., p.49.
[25] Roshkies, op.cit., p. 143.

While Simche and his family lived in Askovitz they had a very good life. But when Czar Nicholas ordered all Jews out of the villages, it hurt Simche badly, for he could not turn his business into money, nor could he move his merchandise, for it was mostly vodka and wine, which he was no longer allowed to sell.

Simche went to rabbi's house to get his geese slaughtered…

The ride was wonderfully smooth on the snowy road. When the tall trees of the thick woods darkened the road, then Simche realized he was halfway home.

To his great astonishment, the horses slowed down almost to a standstill. Then he saw the glittering eyes of a pack of wolves straight ahead, by the road. Simche realized the dangerous situation and, without losing a minute of time, took the whip in his hand and let it fall on the horses. He knew his life was at stake, but there was only one way to get through: fast—faster than the wolves could run.

And calling the horses by their names, Speeder and Save, he continued whipping them, jerking the lines and calling for more speed…But on came the rush of the wolves. Simche picked up a goose and tossed it to the wolves, then a second, a third, a fourth, until there were no more geese left. But one wolf still came after the sleigh with rage and a wide-open mouth. He came right at Simche!

Without thought or time loss, Simche rammed his heavy glove-covered hand deep into the throat. He held the head tight with the other hand, and when he felt the wolf was dead, he pulled his hand out, full of blood. Then Simche fell into his seat, unconscious.

The horses carried him home and when he came to, he was able to tell his story to his weeping wife, mother, and father. An interesting note is that this family was the only Jewish family in this village and their relationships with the villagers was positive. He notes that, "The next day, when the story was told to the peasants, they all went to church, rang the bells and held mass to thank God that He spared them their only Jew, Simche. Then they started to bring geese and ducks to Molke for Passover.[26]

---

[26] Charnofsky, op cit, p.56.

Avrum Gershen (Simche's father) and his family were the only Jews living in Askovitz. They ran the only business in the village for many years. The peasants and their families loved them for the kind things Avrum Gershen did for them. So Avrum Gershen was always remembered by the peasants and their families even at Sunday Mass. They seldom forgot to pray for their Jewish family, asking God to keep them well so they could continue to help the village people.

All through the towns and villages he was loved, admired, and respected. In the towns where Jews lived he was a steady donor to the synagogues, to the bath house, and to poor and sick people…

Rivke, Avrum Gershen's wife, never objected to her husband's philanthropies. Only she kept reminding him that he was giving away too much…She went on to say that even their business was not secure, that there were rumors around that Jews might not be allowed to live in peasant's villages…But Avrum Gershen would explain to her in kind words that what he did was God's command. God gave him enough so that he could help others. And he would be rewarded for his deeds by going to *Gon Aden* (Garden of Paradise). Rivke would go along with him when her time came because she allowed him to do these things. Rivke liked that idea very much and said no more about his being too benevolent.[27]

Reading Simche's encounter with wolves, we hear echoes within our own family history, when we hear that Rosalie was told by Motley, her mother, about being in a sleigh chased by wolves while in the woods outside of Borzna.

What was it like to grow up in a Ukrainian village during the late eighteenth century? What were the forces acting on Pesach, Motley, and their parents? What must the conversations have been about America? How did the decision to emigrate come about?

Although, again, Pesach and Motley didn't leave much of a record for us, others did. There are a number of accounts of Jewish life in the Ukraine, at least one of which is set in the same time frame as Pesach's. And whereas the circumstances are different, we can accept the fact that their lives were probably similar. Jewish customs, especially in towns and villages, would be similar. And sometimes we hear echoes of some of the few experiences that have been passed down from our grandparents. Again, we can listen to the stories from that time and assume that Peter and Martha (for that is what their names became here in America), could at

---

[27] Ibid., p.64.

least relate to them, nod their heads, and say, "Yes, our experience was a little different, but that's the way it was."

Although the Bug is a river now in Poland, the following account gives us a sense of life along a similar river near Borzna. The Desna is the river that flows near Borzna, and there is a smaller river that flows through that city now along with a number of lakes and other bodies of water that would have led to a great deal of winter activity for the Volkovitskys.

> The Bug was also the place where all the people would go to swim. The young men would swim all the way across the river to watch the girls bathing. Everyone swam in the nude, and the men had a place for bathing, and the girls another place. These places were far away from each other, but a good swimmer could swim across to the other side and get directly across from the women's swimming place. No matter how much the women complained to the boys' parents, it did no good. As the rabbi told some of the fathers, if he could swim across he would do it too.

> For washing clothes, there was a special place at one edge of the Bug. There were big stones spread in a row, and each woman would use one for her washing. For a distance one could see a long line of soapy water in the Bug, like a stream of suds.

> The most fun on the Bug came during the winter, when the river would freeze solid…For young Jews and Gentiles this meant skating and sleigh-riding. Most of the time we made our own skates. We took a piece of wood as long as the shoe, put a couple of holes across the width with two strings in to tie to the shoe, and a wire across the length. This made a very good skate, and all we had to do was break it in. When the wire got shiny, the skates were perfect for skating. Our sleds were also homemade. That was easy—even mothers could make sleds for their children. No one ever knew there were so many children in town until the sleigh-riding came along…It was at this time that the Gentile and the Jewish children would mix, and there were no objections from anyone. In fact, one couldn't tell the difference. They all had red cheeks, sparkling eyes, smiling faces, and sportsmanlike feelings— all alike, only some better skaters than others.[28]

---

[28] Ibid., p.137.

In the center of Borzna, and every other town in Ukraine, there was space for the market, typical of the Jewish community there.

> The semi-annual *yarid*, or market day, was a great event in the Ukraine. There were semimonthly and weekly *yarids* held throughout the year, but the semiyearly one was the biggest of them all…You could find horses, cows, goats, pigs, chickens, eggs, wheat corn, oats, potatoes, cabbages, onions, carrots, cucumbers, apples, pears, watermelons,…And for the farmers to buy, there would be shoes, boots, coats, pants, hats, dresses, yardage, groceries, candles, kerosene, grease, oil, soap, wool, cotton, needles, matches…The farmers would also patronize the taverns, where they drank vodka and ate good meals that the townspeople would prepare…The day usually turned into a great carnival of trading and amusements. Tents were pitched for side shows of animals of all sorts, big fat men, tall, skinny men, a half-man and half-horse, flying fishes, and other spectacles. A man accompanied by several girls, dressed in costumes and holding whips in their hands, would call the people to come in and see the wonders. Stands were set up to sell *kvass* and all kinds of candy.

> Beggars dressed in rags would sit on the ground in long rows, playing harmonicas and singing religious songs of mercy…The young boys and girls would walk around the town, holding hands, embracing, singing Ukrainian melodies, stopping for some candy, some kvass, and to watch the side shows. The girls were dressed in white embroidered blouses and full-gathered skirts flowered in striking colors, and they wore kerchiefs on their heads. The boys wore red blouses and bloomer-like trousers. Most of them would be bare-footed…The noises of the animals mixed with the voices of the people calling out their wares for sale would echo through the town from sunrise to dusk. This was a *yarid* in the full sense of the word.[29]

---

[29] Ibid. p.123.

THE END OF THE WORLD—
1899-1900

Occasionally one runs across something that reflects on the thought of the times. We have our events that everyone seems to talk about and have convictions one way or the other, e.g. O.J. Simpson trial or Watergate. Even today, there is the yearly prediction of the end of the world. So here is evidence of this kind of topic gripping the minds and imaginations of Ukrainians just before Pesach begins his exodus to America. Certainly Pesach, Motley, and their families were engaged in discussions about the following.

Everybody talked about the end of the world. Nobody knew who started the story—men, women, and children alike were sure that on a certain date this world of ours would be totally destroyed.

These stories spread like wildfire. They traveled through towns, villages and even big cities. People started to go more to church and to synagogue. The streets were always full of people talking about what was going to happen, and many different decisions were reached. Business was not attended to. The land was completely neglected. Some peasants started to sell their cattle, horses and pigs at very low prices. They [were] offered next to nothing for the stock, and got it. The peasants were saying that they couldn't take the stock with them, but the money they might.

The Jews were left with their merchandise. The shoemakers, capmakers, tailors, and other merchants did no business at all. As the supposed day came nearer this took on a most tragic form, and it seemed as if it really was then end of the world.

The day, the hour, the minute came, and nothing happened. People came out of their hiding places dressed in their best clothes, carrying their harmonicas and other musical instruments, singing Ukrainian songs. The streets were soon full and spirits were high as people prayed and thanked God for changing his mind about destroying the world. Everyone was sure that the prayers had done it.

Those who had sold out their livestock had to start over again. They were almost disappointed; they had been so sure of the end.[30]

---

[30] Ibid., p.221.

DECISION

The decision to emigrate to America is not a spur-of-the-moment action. And in the new Russia of the twentieth century there was much discussion and thought about the New World. And the Volkovitskys must have talked about America and what it might mean to them. One writer of the period wrote about how his mother told him about the United States.

Tomorrow I will tell you about a big country that people talk about...

They call that country America. People go there and claim that they can make a living...You can peddle all kinds of food there and other articles. In fact, one man from Warshilovka is there already. H peddles apples...He sends to his wife every week two dollars, which makes four rubles, and you know what you can do with four rubles? You can feed a big family well and still have some left.

They call America the golden land, full of opportunities for everybody. They say that all through the week you eat white bread there. Meat, potatoes, and vegetables you buy for very little. And most of all, it is a free country. There is no czar. The people choose a new president every four years and all the poor people can vote too as long as they become citizens. They say everybody is equal there. One is not better than another. They say they play music in the streets and children dance. They say that all children must go to school. They say that people from many countries with different religions live together like in a melting pot.

To this country, America, your father and I hope to go some day because of you children.

What have we got here? First, you can say slavery. We are not allowed a free word. I could be sent to Siberia if they knew what I am telling you now...There is nothing to do here. Father struggles, works hard, and he cannot even supply bread for the family.

Worst of all, they hate us here. Anti-Semitism rages high. Don't live here, you can't live there, don't do this, don't do that. You can't travel here and you can't travel there. Schools are for peasant children only.

36

And the poor one-room school with the one teacher and eleven children opens only once or twice a week.

You see, children, here in the country of our birth where we have lived all our lives we have no place and no chance. The only thing left for us to do is to take you to America, the land of the free.

They told us about England. What a wonderful country that was. It was the biggest empire in the world. They said that the sun never sets on English territory. Even America once belonged to England.

In 1903 Mother and Father decided that first Father would go to America, then he would bring the family over...And that is what they did.[31]

One person of Russian ancestry remembers her grandmother singing a lullaby about America:

I remember that my maternal Grandmother would sing us a lullaby entitled "A Russian Lullaby", at least that was what she called it. The words were as follows:

Every night you'll hear them croon a Russian Lullaby.

Just a simple plaintive tune, when baby starts to cry.

Go to sleep my baby, somewhere there may be,

A land that's free, for your and me and a Russian Lullaby.[32]

David Goldman started a lot of people thinking about the issue of leaving family and friends behind. He wrote:

Can folks give me...some perspective on the mentality of young Jews in a big city like Odessa in the first years of the 20th century who were prepared to leave everyone in their family behind forever? I know the idea of the solid Jewish family is problematic. It was an age with no

---

[31] Ibid., p. 190.

[32] Charlotte A. Showel, Tracing an old tune, e-mail, 28 May 1999, Las Vegas, NV.

email, no international telephone service or airlines. That was their agenda to take such a drastic move, even risking being cut off from their entire family forever.

My great-grandmother left Odessa in 1907 because her fiance had left with his whole family for New York in 1905 (probably because of the turmoil there at the time). She was only about 15 and he was 20. Both were intellectuals. He had met her because he studied with her father, who was an official rabbi in a nearby town. Years later she regretted leaving her family behind.... She never saw her parents again, though she wrote letters, especially to an older sister who she also never saw again even though. The two wrote to each other for almost 60 years! My great-grandmother even left behind small siblings who she of course never really knew either. She didn't manage to keep up with the rest of the family, and there was some sad stories back home, especially during World War I and never talked much about her family with her children and grandchildren. There was one occasion that they thought they could bring over her older sister, who was a widow. My great-grandmother supposedly didn't want to do it because she thought her sister was a Communist and would create problems for her own family in Canada! Imagine, losing an opportunity like that for fear of a 70 year old communist widow![33]

Regarding reasons for leaving family and friends behind, one person wrote:

There were a lot of reasons, including freedom of religion, safety, economic betterment, and love. Many parents urged their children to emigrate to have a better life, or to save their sons from the draft. After a pogrom, or news of a pogrom, there would be a push to go somewhere where there would be no pogroms. Many, even in the big cities, lived in terrible poverty without hope of improving their lot. Others left to join loved ones in the new countries. The US was called the "Goldena

---

[33] David Goldman, Leaving Family Behind in Russia, e-mail,7 May 1999.

Medina", the Golden Land, where a person could make a life as a Jew and become wealthy.

As they left, they may or may not have realized they were seeing some relatives for the last time. They may have hoped the rest of the family would join them some time in the future. Telephones, email, airplanes, were not even dreamed about. They knew letters would be the only contact, and perhaps future visits. If their lives were wonderful, they probably wouldn't have left. Let's face it; most of us are here because our Great Great Whoevers wanted more than they could expect to have where they were. More in terms of freedom of religion, jobs and opportunity. They paid more than the cost of transportation in terms of those left behind. Pioneers in any time or place do the same.[34]

Another person wrote:

From my grandparents' letters to each other and from other family members (ca1910-1922), they left for reasons like extreme poverty, total lack of opportunity in Russia to support oneself, the danger of being Jewish—very real, not just in textbooks. My grandmothers' sisters cite curfews and roundups in Kiev, the Beiliss case (one of their uncles was also arrested and later released on a bloodmobile charge), pogroms and unemployment. My grandmother referred to "my damned Kiyev where I can't sleep peacefully at night". She was sure she would in America. One of my mother's aunts carried a scar on her back from a Cossack's saber, a memento of the pogroms of 1905.

Sounds to me like a compelling reason to get out of Dodge! And don't forget that the old parents often encouraged their children to leave, sacrificing the prospect of having their children in their lives for the chance that their children would not only live, but thrive.

---

[34] Shelley Volk, <u>Leaving Family Behind in Russia</u>, e-mail, 7 May 1999, Chicago, Illinois

In addition, there was often every expectation that the whole family would eventually come over. My grandfather and 6 sisters made it here, the last sister and the elderly parents died of typhus during World War I. On the other hand, my grandmother was the only one to make it here—again, the war and the Russian revolution intervened. By then it was too late. She arrived in 1913, just before the storm, thank God.

How did they do it? They suffered greatly. They resolutely looked forward and kept their pain to themselves. To talk about it accomplished nothing (i.e., didn't bring their family to the US) and reminded them of their sorrow. They coped, and cried in private.

My grandfather's one burning desire was to get to this country. Nothing would stand in his way, and he felt responsible for helping to bring the rest of his sisters, too. We cannot comprehend just how horrible conditions were, our lives are so different. Poverty, illness, poor hygiene, repression, the draft, we have no idea what that is like. But I bless the day they left Russia and came here. Ten years ago when we were resettling Russian refugees, I watched them get off the plane and thought, there but for the grace of God...our forebears suffered and sacrificed so that I would be on the receiving end of that immigration, rather than coming off the plane. They were real heroes, as were the family members left behind.[35]

It was 1904 when Pesach came to America. We can only imagine what discussions led to this choice, who agreed, who disagreed, who could only remain silent.

When these discussions took place in Pesach's family, he was in the czar's army. And even though he apparently was in a military band (according to my father, he played the clarinet), he faced being sent into Manchuria to fight in the Russo-Japanese War. Some understanding of how the decision to emigrate can be gained from this account of how this war forced Pesach to begin thinking about leaving possibly as early as 1901.

---

[35] Louise Goldstein, <u>Leaving Family Behind in Russia</u>, e-mail, 8 May 1999.

Nineteen hundred and one was the coldest winter in fifty years in the Ukraine. It was so cold that water froze in seconds outside, and the windows were solidly iced.

Mother kept two fires going all the time, and the house was not warm. We dressed in our coats in the house, and for the night Mother covered us with everything she had to keep us warm. In fact, many nights we were all on the brick-built stove. As the top was flat, you could sleep on it while the fire went on in the stove all the time.

Father couldn't leave the house for almost four weeks, and he started to worry about the wood and straw supply for burning. Also, food had dwindled. The street was free of people. It seemed that no one walked out…The Sunday *yarid* (market day) was not held. No one came. Stores were closed. The town was cut off from everything…One day toward the end of January, it was a nice day. The sun was out in its full warmth shining on the white-covered town of Warshilovka, and around noon we heard the church bells ringing, and soon after saw people starting to come out to the street. There was a big sleigh drawn by four horses …with a big picture of the czar hung high on the sleigh and two men dressed in very heavy fur coats and big fur hats over the ears, fur gloves, and big pushten (boots) made out of heavy warm material. They were calling the people to the center of town to read a proclamation to them. All the people could not come out, for they had no such warm clothes to wear, but a good many came out to find out what was happening. The proclamation was read that Russia was facing war with Japan; that every town, village, and city must be ready for that time.

The demand was first that all people of military age should join the army. All citizen-subjects should start now to economize, and all workers should make more hats, shoes, and coats.

The next year a long winter set in, although not so severe as the last one. But winter in the Ukraine is nothing to push away with one hand. It is winter for six months or more, and it is snow on the ground and frozen windows. It is sleigh riding and it is winter.[36]

---

[36] Charnofsky, op.cit., p.111.

The Russo-Japanese War began in earnest in February 1904—over 30,000 Jews were sent to the Far East. Pesach was already a soldier. The enlistment period was thirty years—and Jewish soldiers were marked for conversion to Christianity. It was only a matter of time before he, too, would be sent.

The year before, 1903, was also not an auspicious time. The Jews had been expelled from Kiev. There were pogroms in Kishinef and Homel. The world heard about Kishinef—certainly it made the rounds in Borzna. It was April. 50,000 Jews were killed or injured for two days. Jewish shops were plundered.

In the early part of 1904, Rebecca was born. The family was growing; one couldn't really support a family playing the clarinet in the army (for the next 25 years), fearing being sent off to war, anti-Jewish sentiment growing in the community—all this was obviously weighing on their thought. Friends had already left for America. It seems that one of Motley's brothers had left. Perhaps they had corresponded. Perhaps they were waiting to help him should he come to America. Yes! He'd do it…They'd do it!

The decision to leave is one thing. The actual act is something else. Pesach and Motley must have planned very carefully. In addition to the considerations given in the preceding accounts, they had other concerns. What about his parents? What about her parents? How would Motley and the girls come to him? And when? What faith!

Again, we don't know exactly what transpired. But, again, we can imagine it through the eyes of another Ukrainian family undergoing a similar experience at almost the same time and place:

> The struggle for a living was too great and hard. The danger of living in Russia, the anti-Semitism, the persecution of the Jews became unbearable. So Simche and Molke, as usual on Saturday night…discussed their mere existence, their struggle to earn a piece of bread, and the difficulties of raising their children in such terrible poverty and under frightful anti-Semitism.

> The boys were getting big. What could they expect in Russia? What opportunities were awaiting them in Russia. But if they were in America, in the golden land, everything would be open for them. Molke agreed, and encouraged Simche and told him that she would manage until he could establish himself in America and be able to take her and the children over there too. They made the decision that they must make a break.

> But traveling cost money. Where could they get at least one hundred rubles? So Molke started to figure what she could get from her furniture.

…For the seat in the Synagogue they could get ten rubles…Then her jewelry, her copper pots, her brass ornaments, the hand-embroidered tablecloths and some beautiful bedspreads—if she would take those to Herschel, the moneylender, and give them to him for security, he might lend her fifty rubles.

When Molke saw Hershel, he was willing to lend her sixty rubles, but she would have to pay back ten for the advance interest. Molke was happy to do that, and so in one day she raised the hundred rubles. So they called for the travel agent and all the arrangements were made to leave in ten days. It would take that long to get ready.

And in ten days, Simche was on his way to the golden land with high hopes for a great future.[37]

Finally, this day also comes for Pesach. We don't know exactly when. Was he in Borzna? Probably not, since he was in the army, and my father indicates that he went AWOL. One can only imagine how that occurred. What connections did he have to make? Where did he go? What was he risking—what were the penalties for deserters if he got caught? Simche wasn't in the army. Molke apparently didn't need to be circumspect about raising the money for passage. The Russo-Japanese War was beginning, and Jewish men were being rounded up to fight there. Already being in the army didn't bode well for Pesach's future. In addition to anti-Semitism and economic difficulties, there was the immediate threat of being sent to Manchuria. And this factor presented another problem—saying goodbye.

How do you plan to go AWOL and at the same time say goodbye? This might be part of the pain that forced Pesach to not speak much of his past. He probably couldn't speak freely of his plans. Probably this situation forced him to simply disappear one day and leave the explanation for others to make once he was on his way.

How does one say good-bye to one's wife of only two years, to family, to friends, to one's home? How do the ones who remain behind say good-bye? Pesach doesn't say. But others do. Their feelings are universal. One immigrant wrote,

---

[37] Ibid., p.223.

In the evening when we were alone together my mother would make me sit on her footstool, and while her deft fingers manipulated the knitting-needles she would gaze into my eyes as if she tried to absorb enough of me to last her for the coming months of absence. "You will write us, dear?" she kept asking continually. "And if I should die when you are gone, you will remember me in your prayers."

At the moment of departure, when the train drew into the station, she lost control of her feelings. As she embraced me for the last time her sobs become violent and father had to separate us. There was despair in her way of clinging to me which I could not then understand. I understand now. I never saw her again.[38]

Another writes,

With an aching heart I departed in the dark from Krivoy Rog, where I had passed so many bright, spiritually rich moments...We came upon a party of my best friends. They had traveled all the way to that point in order to take leave of me...And what a leave-taking that was! When we fell each upon the other's neck, we were unable to tear ourselves loose, and the tears of both commingled and seared our very hearts and souls. And when the train began to move, a few ran frantically after the train and cried, "Why are you forsaking us?"

The most terrible ordeal was my departure from Pereshtchepina. My parents-in-law, now quite old, cried aplenty during the few days we stayed with them; and at the last moment, when we were already seated in the wagons that were to carry us to the railroad station, and all stood around us and wailed as at a funeral, I saw the aged couple stand leaning against each other, white as chalk, motionless like two figures carved on a monument of stone and joined together; not a word, not a tear, but only four widely-opened, frightened eyes staring glassily at the wagons that were taking away all that was dear to them. One looks that

---

[38] Howe, op.cit. p.34

way at his children only when he never expects to see them again. That look haunted me for a long time.

An account was also given by a fellow Jewish genealogy researcher in Australia (via e-mail) which gives a similar story:

My grandfather Rev. Menachem Mendel Gildin left Beshincovichi, in Belarus, first with two sons in 1900 to be followed by my mother Louise Gilden, and five other children. He left my Great Grandfather Rabbi Avram Yisroel Gildenson. He left because of poverty, conscription, and pogroms.

I have his diary in which he describes the parting at the railway station. It translates:

We sat in silence waiting for the train to arrive. But when the train arrived, I could not move. And so we sat as three more trains came and went. We shared a small piece of rather hard bread. We were both cold, but I kept thinking that I would never see him again. And I could see in his eyes that he knew that also. It was nearing time for Mincha/Miriv. With a heavy heart I boarded the next train. As the train pulled out I felt my heart would break. He did not move and at last I lost sight of him. He was my Rabbi, my teacher and my father and I was leaving him for good.

He never saw him again. The Rabbi died in 1915.

Just one of many similar stories.[39]

Why do parents do such things? On the one hand, saying "goodbye" to one's children, knowing they would not return. On the other hand knowing that they were leaving for a better life, an experience that would transcend what would remain for them if they stayed. In a newspaper editorial about the drug wars that rage currently in a South American country, a father puts it succinctly: "As a parent, you do what you can for them, you do it before you think about your own life."[40]

---

[39] David Frey, e-mail: 8 May 1999, Victoria, Australia

[40] Howard LaFranchi, *It took a village to save their children*, The Christian Science Monitor, p.1,10/30/00.

Apparently, neither Motley nor Pesach spoke a great deal about their life in Borzna. Even about relatives who remained behind. No one heard or knew about Pesach's family. He must have had brothers, sisters, aunts and uncles. Yet he never spoke of them. At least none of his children remembers this. It provokes thought to wonder about why. Was there guilt about leaving? Were they murdered in a pogrom? Was leaving so painful that one couldn't "recall"? When Motley left, it was forever. In these present times, families move across the country, even to other countries. But they return for visits; family members visit them. When Pesach said goodbye, everyone knew it was for good. When Motley left, parents, grandparents, cousins, aunts all knew they would never see her or the children again. Nor would she ever see them again. It was like they were to die. And if later Pesach and his wife heard of the deaths of these loved ones, perhaps it was too much to talk about them.

Others have written about this lack of communication about what was being left behind. One person wrote, "I thought that when I left he country it was forever and that I would never see my parents again. This was a typical experience for many people. You left, and for you the people you were leaving behind were as good as dead. They were alive, but you lost them the way you lose people when they die."[41]

Perhaps we remember these pioneers not only for their courage in facing a new land but also for their sacrifice in leaving. Perhaps these sacrifices "haunted them for a long time."

Pesach's Father, Israel Baruch   Motley's Father,   Motley's Mother
                                    Arya Leib

---

[41] David Remnich, *Lenin's Tomb*, p. 21.

THE VOYAGE

- - - - - - - - - -

On his way, Simche dreamed out his plans—laid them out beautifully. He had heard how easy it was to make money in New York. That was how people talked about it; actually, they said that there was money on the streets of New York. All you had to do was pick it up. But Simche knew differently…He knew you had to work and be honest, and God would help. He also knew that he was not an ignorant man. He knew the Torah…He could also write and figure. He was sure that he would have no trouble in making a nice living and saving enough to bring Molke and the children over very soon. And the closer he got to the end of the journey, the more excited he got.

Here was the Statue of Liberty, and there was New York with its tall, heaven-high buildings. And here was the Island of Tears, Ellis Island. And as the boat docked, the word went around that you had to have ten dollars or someone to call for you. Simche had none.[42]

- - - - - - - - - -

From 1904 Ship List

---

[42] Charnofsky, op.cit., p.224.

Probably the most written-about experience of immigrants of this time is the trip itself. Unfortunately, all we know about Pesach Volkovitsky is that he left on the steamship *St. Louis* from Southampton, England on July 9, 1904 and arrived in New York on July 18, 1904, a voyage of over two weeks.

St. Louis (1895) American Line.

> Built by Wm. Cramp & Sons Shipbuilding & Engineering Co., Philadelphia, Pa. Tonnage 11,629. Dimensions: 535 "x 63' Twin-screw, 21 knots...Launched November 12, 1894...Equipped with 10 boilers, which had a total of 64 furnaces. Passengers 320 first, 210 second, 800 third. Maiden Voyage: New York-Southampton, June 5, '1895. Renamed (a) **Louisville** (1917) United States Government, (b) **St. Louis** (1920). Served as a troopship in First World War. She caught fire while refitting in 1920. The scuttled liner was refloated, but the rusting burned-out liner remained tied up in New York for four years. Finally towed to Italy to be dismantled by shipbreakers in 1925 Sister ship: **St. Paul** [43] *(See below for Motley and children.)*

There is fertile ground for imagination. For example, how did he get to England? Did he go overland through Eastern Europe? Or North? Actually, a major route was south to Odessa and the Black Sea, sailing east through the Mediterranean and then up to England. Both my father and mother had said that they thought the Volkoffs came from the Odessa region. Knowing now that Borzna was their ancestral home, I can imagine that this geographic area might have been mentioned if it provided an exit from what was then Russia. He may even have stayed in the area a while. An e-mail asks this question:

> Is anyone aware of how soldiers in the Imperial ("Czar's") Army around 1904 would have accomplished leaving for the US? My grandfather (born 1877 in Odessa) was already in the army, emigrated alone (probably first to New York, then Boston) and a year or so later was joined

---

[43] Eugene Smitn, <u>Passenger Ships of the World</u>, p. 233.

by his wife and children. Would he have had to have left "secretly" with organized help? Was there a most common place of departure? I would appreciate any clues.

Stories I have heard from my own family included false passports, either forged, or purchased from a relative of a deceased person. One female relative made dresses and wigs for the young boys and walked with them from Lutsk til they were able to smuggle across the border at Brody under cover of darkness. Others just paid their way out and rode across the border on wagons but then had to walk quite a distance. They had to be very careful to walk in each others footsteps (in the snow) so as not to arouse the suspicions of the "guards".

When I first started doing genealogy and talking to the older relatives, these stories were always mentioned as an 'aside' comment—somewhat of an embarrassment. It seemed that they did not really want to talk about doing something that was—in our eyes—illegal or dishonest. These things were never talked about once they arrived in the U.S. because they were afraid that if they were "found out"—they would be sent back!

My grandfather also left for US in 1904. I do not know about his route, but I heard stories as follows when growing up: My grandfather used his mother's maiden surname, BRICHKE, as he first deserted the army and had to only see his family at night in a dark room so that he would not be caught.

In 1904 was an attempted communist revolution which failed. In our case, my grandfather was proud that he was a Bolshevik and helped pass out Marxist literature as part of the revolution attempt. But he had to leave for several reasons then, as a Jew and a Bolshevik and a deserter he was in big danger and the family too. He was the oldest son.

The story goes that he escaped in a "hay wagon" which could have been arranged through one of the underground groups. The story is that before crossing whatever border he crossed, soldiers thrusted pitch forks into the hay to make sure no one was escaping and somehow my grandfather made it relatively unscathed. My grandfather kept the assumed surname for a long time in the US before changing his name to our family's real name

Pesach's wife and children remained behind in Borzna. A year later, they, too, repeated his adventure, leaving Liverpool in May 1905, arriving in New

York on May 29 aboard the steamship *St. Paul*. And whereas he came alone, Motley had to bring the children—five-year old Sara, two-year old Bekie, and one-year old Florence.

Much has been written about the trip by others. A few made the trip in cabins in comparative luxury. Many more, including the Volkovitskys, spent their time in steerage. This was literally hellish. Although the steamship lines advertised a trip of less than a week, with good food and comfortable lodgings, the truth turned out to be something entirely different. Often after one week they had only progressed half-way. The length of these Atlantic crossings was more like ten to fifteen days of constant misery. The meals by that time were barely edible, usually soggy rye bread and herring. Steerage quarters, which were always below deck were crowded, often thousands of people in a room 6-8 feet high with a blanket on a rope to separate the men from the women and children.

> With no portholes, little ventilation, and skimpy toilet facilities, the smell was appalling. Most passengers didn't wash; the few that did had to brave the cold ocean water that ran from faucets in the steerage washroom. Many passengers believed that eating garlic on bread warded off seasickness. That made steerage even smellier…Many were seasick. "I couldn't lift my head for four days," a Czech immigrant later recalled. "I thought I'd never see the United States." When the weather turned bad and the immigrants were indeed tempest-tossed they were unable to get up onto the deck to vomit overboard. In stormy weather the steerage hatchway door was locked…to make sure that no passenger reached deck and got swept overboard. Since the only drinking water was available on deck, stormy weather brought thirst as well as seasickness.

> Inside the steerage cabin there were bunks, two or three tiers high, equipped with meager mattresses populated by lice. Women with babies made sure they got a lower bunk. They had to sleep with their arms around their children who might easily roll out of bed while the boat was rocking. Beneath them the noisy engine was constantly pounding.[44]

> All the steerage berths were of iron, the framework forming two tiers and having but a low partition between the individual berths. Each bunk contained a mattress filled with straw…there were no pillows. A short and light-weight white blanket was the only covering provided.

---

[44] Susan Jonas, *Ellis Island, Echoes from a Nation's Past*, p17.

Two washrooms were provided for the use of steerage. The first morning out I took special care to inquire for the women's wash room. One of the crew directed me to a door bearing the sign Washroom for Men. Within were both men and women. Thinking I had been misdirected, I proceeded to the other washroom. This bore no label and was likewise used by both sexes. The small basins served as a dishpan for washing greasy tins, as a laundry tub for soiled handkerchiefs and clothing, and as a basin for shampoos, and without receiving any special cleaning. It was the only receptacle for use in the case of seasickness.

During these twelve days in the steerage I lived in a disorder and in surroundings that offended every sense. Only the fresh breezes from the sea overcame the sickening odors. Everything was dirty, sticky, and disagreeable to the touch. Every impression was offensive.[45]

For the privilege of experiencing this introduction to the free world, they had paid around thirty-five dollars. Children paid half price; infants were free. And for most East Europeans, certainly the Volkoffs, this was their first experience with an ocean. Probably it didn't take long for many of these travelers to become convinced they had made a dreadful mistake. Perhaps this was but one of the reasons the Volkovitskys rarely talked about their life in Borzna nor the difficulties they faced in getting to the New World.

A number of people have written of the courage of these immigrants to make this trip to the New World. One person writes about her mother and grandmother:

My grandmother came from Tyczyn where she didn't have indoor plumbing or any of the amenities we take for granted. She traveled, alone, to Hamburg to get on a ship for New York City with a nine month old child, my mother. She brought along a lamp with which to heat baby bottles, which was against the rules because it needed a lighted wick. How did she get away with it? She strapped it to her leg!!

To look at my grandmother, who died 30 years ago, you would never have thought she had the gumption. When you think of what we go through just to get away for a weekend you have to give a big pat on the back to our forebears who crossed lands and seas to get here.

G-d give them peace.[46]

---

[45] William S. Tift, *Ellis Island,*
[46] Dorothy Auerbach Rivers, <u>Courage of our ancestors</u>, e-mail, 1/23/01.

The steamship companies were enjoying wonderful profits. The liners could hold almost 2,000 steerage passengers. The cost of the trip was met by the fees paid by the two cabin classes. Steerage was total profit. The cost spent for steerage passengers was minimal; one immigrant took only sixty cents a day to feed.[47] It wasn't until 1910 that a congressional committee was established to investigate the conditions of steerage travel.

According to some accounts the cost was around $20. One person writes that in an autobiography a cousin says that in 1905, there were pogroms in Akkerman, Odessa, and Kashira and most of the Jews were trying to get out and come to this country. Shipping companies (the German and the Swiss particularly) had, at that time, a competition and were selling tickets on the boat for $10 apiece[48] Today that doesn't seem so much, but $20 then converts to almost $360 today (1999).

If the *St. Louis* and *St. Paul* were our *Mayflowers*, one wonders if the Pilgrims might not have had a better deal.[49]

---

[47] Thomas Dunne, *Ellis Island.*

[48] Bernard Margolis, <u>The cost of a transatlantic cruise in 1905</u>., e-mail, 2/26/01.

[49] For an excellent account of the conditions of steerage and the ordeal that faced the Jews (or almost any other immigrants at this time), see *World of Our Fathers* by Irving Howe, Chapter 2, especially pages 39-42.

St. Paul

St. Louis

THE ARRIVAL

They probably had a poor grasp of English. They were entering a culture which was just beginning, and in spite of the hope it inspired and the opportunity it presented, it must have been daunting. One immigrant, a Rumanian, wrote:

> Becoming an American is a spiritual adventure of the most volcanic variety…To be born in one world and to grow to manhood there, to be thrust then into the midst of another with all one's racial heritage, with one's likes and dislikes, aspirations and prejudices, and to be abandoned to the task of adjusting within one's own being the clash of opposed systems of culture, tradition, and social convention—if this is not heroic tragedy, I should like to be told what it is.[50]

So, here they were in America, these two brave pioneers. They weren't the first, and they certainly wouldn't be the last. But they were OUR first and last. They wouldn't say much about their past; perhaps there was much they wanted to forget. Yet it was in Borzna that they grew up. In Borzna their relatives were living and were buried. There were mothers and fathers, brothers and sisters, grandparents, friends. There were the memories of childhood. They had left a land where there was hatred and fear and poverty. Yet, there is something that loves in the familiar aura of a place where one was a child.

In a wonderful account of a Holocaust escape from a Ukrainian *shtetl* there is a poignant story. Manya, her husband, and their baby were in a boat being smuggled out of Ukraine. During their journey on a cold November night she could see lights on the Rumanian shore, with gypsy music in the air. She then writes,

---

[50] Marshall B. Davidson, *Life in America: Vol. II*, p.411.

Turning back to the Russian shore, she saw quite another sight. A small schtetl was ablaze. Petlura's men had no doubt visited the village: their signatures were glowing against the blackened sky.

"Good riddance," she whispered, shaking a fist at the shore—at the homeland that regarded her as a despised intruder. Then she raised her hand to her lips and gently blew a kiss to all that was familiar and loved.

"Good-bye, schtetl, forever."[51]

And for Pesach and Motley, it was also a defiant, "Good riddance"; then perhaps a tender and heartfelt, "Good-bye *schtetl*, forever."

We cannot now ask them about their life there. We can read about life in other towns. Yet we can still do something—we can go there ourselves. We can visit to see for ourselves what they saw and perhaps to play "Walter Mitty". While researching this book, I wondered about "returning" to our "home town." In 1990 I did.

- - - - - - - - - -

RODINA
A Trip to Borzna

Rodina is a concept that is not typical for Americans (except the Native Americans). It is a feeling that accompanies the term "Motherland" and seems to me to involve a deeply ingrained love for the land of one's beginnings. It is not really involved with nationalism or even patriotism. I love my country. I am a patriot. Yet there is something that stirs me about the Ukraine, its history and its people. I want to touch it—to feel it. It has led me to study the Russian language

---

[51] Bettyanne Gray, *Manya's Story: Faith and Survival in Revolutionary Russia*, p.113.

so I can read its great Russian literature and folk music and something stirs within me. Why? Perhaps it is some grain of *Rodina* within which is some inner memory calling out unsatisfied until I "return" to Borzna.

Ever since I discovered that my three aunts and grandparents immigrated from a town in the Ukraine, I knew I wanted to try to visit it. My efforts at developing a family tree and working on a family history that contained more than genealogical vital statistics kept drawing me to this goal of traveling to this "hometown". My father began his autobiography with the statement that his father "never played fiddle for the Czar, but he did play the clarinet in the Czar's army band." Aunt Marion recalled that the town's name was Borzna. I could hardly wait to locate this on a map. It was a small dot (so small it isn't on many maps), close to the Desna River about 100 miles northeast of the ancient Ukrainian capital, Kiev.

According to the *Encyclopedia of Ukraine* Borzna was founded in 1633 in Chernihiv oblast (similar to a state.) The population in 1897 was 12,000. In 1970 it was 12,200. Its lack of growth is attributable to its distance from the railway (14 kilometers). It has a brick factory, a lumber-processing factory, and a food industry.[52]

Imagination cries out with questions demanding answers: What is it like? What kind of countryside surrounds it? (Aunt Rose recalls her mother telling of being on a sleigh in the winter woods with a pack of wolves chasing her.) What is the town like? What do the people look like? Are there any relatives still there? Is it even possible to get there? During most of my life Russia was a land that generally was off-limits to non-Russians. And even for most Russians travel was restricted. Yet events unfolded during the 1980's that made the opportunity more achievable.

And so, with all of this developing within me, an opportunity presented itself in 1990 to live with a family in Kiev for a week as part of a Homestay program. It would give me a chance to practice my Russian, experience a cultural exchange, see Russia in a way not possible on a packaged tour and...perhaps to get to Borzna? How? Was the road paved? I didn't know. I would need a car. Could I drive in Russia? As this experience began, I was determined to try. Perhaps I'd rent a car and drive there!

---

[52] Kubijovyc, Volodymyr (Editor), *Encyclopedia of Ukraine.*

At least my experience was not like another's who was returning to Moscow—a reporter who was writing a book about the period after the fall of the USSR. His wife's family had some time previous fled Russia. Her grandmother had refused to speak of it or her past. Just before he left for his assignment she said, "I hope you come home once in a while, because I don't think I could visit you there."[53]

The director of the Homestay program said I was limited by my visa to within 25 miles of Kiev. If I extended this, I was on my own. Still, my primary goal would be seeing Borzna. Was it worth renting a car and winding up in Fortovo Prison like the German who flew his plane into Red Square? There was no one, once I arrived in Moscow (where I was to spend my first week), who felt reaching my goal was impossible, and this was encouraging. But I was not prepared for what happened on the train that was taking me to Kiev. Because I wanted to practice my Russian, I was assigned to a sleeping car with a Russian citizen.

The reporter I mentioned previously tells of speaking about his three-year assignment with a centenarian who had escaped Russia earlier. He said, "You must be crazy. We almost got killed going out and you, meshuggah, you want to go back in."[54]

I wanted to go back—at least for just a day.

The following is from the journal I was keeping of my experiences.

- - - - - - - - - -

Friday, July 6, 1990

...I am in a compartment with a man who is not with our Homestay group. After conversing briefly in Russian, I discover he speaks very broken English. He is involved with selling computer equipment in the USSR. "Where are you from?", I asked. "Seal Beach, California", he replies! He has lived there with his wife and five-year old son for two months. He, Alex, has returned with his wife, Natasha, to Kiev to see their parents. He is Jewish and is trying to get his parents to emigrate to the

---

[53] Remnick, p.23.
[54] Ibid., p.22.

USA. (Her parents did not want to leave, and I get the impression she herself was not too anxious to leave.) He asks the inevitable question about why I was in the USSR. I showed him my folder of photographs, including those of Peter and Martha, and explain my desire to get to Borzna (showing him a copy of a map identifying its location.) "I will help you get there", he said. He can get a car, and if I call him after I arrive "things can be arranged, perhaps Monday" (this is Friday night). My feelings are difficult to express—first, excitement at the first really positive step at reaching my goal—perhaps I really am going to get there. Second, doubt and trepidation. After all, I really did not know this man or his motives. I asked him why he was willing to help me and he said it sounded interesting and it would be a good trip. I have some concern, but at the same time it is the best offer yet.

We talk until 2:00 A.M. and finally, exhausted, we get ready for bed. This promises to be an interesting time ahead. It is itself like a dream, for here I am, falling asleep to the clickety-clack of the Kiev Train, traveling (not smoothly) through the Ukraine, taking me closer and closer to…Borzna.

Saturday, July 7, 1990

I wake up early and want desperately to look outside. It is light but the shade is drawn and I do not want to wake Alexei. Finally he stirs and I am able to get my first view of the Ukrainian countryside. It is truly beautiful. Green—many flowers—expansive fields of wheat can be seen when the forest parts. Along the tracks are many small plots of vegetables—beans, squash (what kind? all I can see as we speed past are the tell-tale yellow flowers)—some corn, and sunflowers, cabbage, etc. Alexei notes my excitement but says, "This does not appeal to me—especially after Chernobyl." Also, although he has indicated he is not an actively practicing Jew, he says, "I am JEWISH—not Russian."[55] Yet, I still want to soak this in as much as I can. After spending a week in Moscow, the countryside appears like a drink of fresh water (even if it is radioactive).

---

[55] This is in contrast to the following from a biography of Sholom Aleichem: "Treated like stepchildren, limited to the outer fringes…the Russian Jews still loved their fatherland, and the Czar of all the Russias was, for better or worse, their czar." Marie Waike-Goldberg, *My Father; Sholom Aleichem*, p.26-27.

Then, I see my first Ukrainians! People working in a field—traditionally dressed! A man in a white cap, scything—*babushki* (grandmothers) with the traditional scarves on their heads sitting on benches waiting for a train to arrive. Alex says, "We are now not far from Borzna."

On Sunday I was able to reach Alex by phone and arranged to meet him early Monday morning.

Monday, July 9, 1990

This morning I am going to BORZNA!

We will leave at 6:00 so am up at 5:00…. It is difficult to describe one's feelings at a time like this. I have come to the USSR for this day. I want to be as sponge-like as I can, and yet I know I will miss much. What will it be like?…Alexei is late. Finally he arrives. In the car is his wife who wants to do some shopping in Borzna. The car is borrowed. During the trip out of the city we pass lines of perhaps 80-90 cars waiting for a gas station to open—maybe it will, maybe it won't. Alex says that on a trip to Rostov he waited a week to get gas. Perhaps noting a concerned expression on my face, he assures me that we have a full tank. I wonder how he got it, whose car this was, where we were going, and perhaps would I disappear never to be seen again. I decide to take it one step at a time and get back to being a sponge.

The road is a large one (by Russian standards)—the main road between Kiev and Moscow. There are two lanes on either side. The countryside is beautiful, not at all like our native grasslands in the Midwest that stretch on and on. Here are wide fields of wheat, yes, but they are surrounded by dense borders of forest, mostly conifers and birch. There are many beautiful flowers. (Alexei, again, does not find this as pleasant as I—he thinks only about Chernobyl). The road is good, and Alex drives very fast—maybe 100 kilometers per hour. I look occasionally at the road map he has brought and see Borzna and surrounding country. He says at one point, "We are now only twenty miles from Borzna." I let my mind wander to that first day I found Borzna on a map and wondered if I would ever be able to be there. Suddenly we pass a bus stop shelter on the side of the road. On its frame is printed " Борзна " [Borzna in Cyrillic.) It's at times like these when you wonder, "Dare I go further?" After several hundred yards is a small road crossing the highway—leading to Borzna. We turn north and almost immediately come upon a large structure with the name

БОРЗНА on it with a large symbolic shield. We stop to look and take pictures. I suppose this is my first time actually stepping on the soil of my "home town".

We drive on into the town itself. There are many old homes decorated with colorful wooden carvings around the windows and roofs—just like one sees in pictures of rural Russian towns. We see a young woman walking along the road and stop to ask her if she knows any Volkovitskys in the town. She says there are three and agrees to take us to the first. She gets in and off we go. She directs us to a house where Alex, being more fluent than I, gets out to speak with the inhabitants. I have a chance now to talk with this "Borznian". Again, how can I describe my feelings about talking with this individual? Events begin happening almost too fast. I want to stretch this out—to think—to absorb. After a few minutes, Alex returns with the man and wife who live there. They say that the Volkovitskys in the town are not Jewish—and that V. is not a Jewish name, it is Ukrainian. They said there were only three Jews left in Borzna and perhaps they could help us.

We park in what could be described as the town square...and walk to the house of a woman named Fannye. A lady, perhaps in her seventies, appears at the door...She does not know the name Volkovitsky—Yes, the last Sovitsky died three years ago. He was a glassmaker and his daughter had moved to Kharkov. She cried as she described what happened to the Jews in Borzna. In 1942 there were over 200 Jews in Borzna. They were hiding underground. A Ukrainian told the Nazis their location. They were rounded up, taken to a field, and shot. She was out of town at that time—her sister (who now lives in Brooklyn with her daughter!), escaped just before they came, naked, out into the winter cold.

Seeing the sensitivity here, it was difficult to ask many more questions. "Was there a Synagogue here?" "Yes, but now it sometimes serves as a fish market." She sent us there with a small boy from Baku who was living with her. It is a large, old building. I can't help but feel that here was a place that Pesach would have known and worshipped at. Again, I wished for time to just look...and think...and feel. Alex and I walk around it, and we agree it is a sad place. And yet, it still stands, a large building with an enormous history, and its proud soul is still there for those who know...

We then stop at the home of Lena. This wonderful lady appears to be decades older than Fannye. She is very short (not even 5'). She confirms what we have heard. I ask her about a Jewish cemetery. She says there is one, although she doesn't like to go there because of the desecration…Before we leave I asked if I could take her picture. She smiled "yes" and tried to smooth her unruly white hair with her hands as we stepped outside. Both the homes we've visited were very old and had a strong musty odor within. I didn't notice anything that suggested that this was a Jewish residence although both were dark inside. As we leave she says significantly, "The earth smells for me." Soon there will be no Jews in Borzna…

We drive off to find the cemetery. This is now very rural country—mud roads with deep ruts often filled with water. Alex is driving this poor car as though it were a jeep. I pity the owner after this trip. I see many babushkas following herds of cattle or shepherding flocks of geese. These people are not hungry. There were many geese and ducks and chickens. It is like a scene out of <u>Fiddler on the Roof.</u> Finally we find the location and walk over to some markers we see in the distance. They are surrounded by a metal fence but are mostly recent. All are located at the edge of a field and number no more than eight or nine. Where are the older graves? A woman walks by and we inquire about these. She says that this was all that is left—the main part has been plowed under! I can see why Lena doesn't like to come out here. My original motive for learning Russian was to be able to read the markers here. As we stand on this field Alex says that we are probably standing on the spot. I know now that the Synagogue-Fishmarket has become their last remaining monument.

- - - - - - - - - -

During this experience, my wife wrote the following during this trip:

WAITING
Send hummingbirds
To grace my day,
A buttercup or two,
The scent of grass,
Of clover sweet,
Also, a note from you!

While you're away
My plain gray day
Will need such light as these
To read thereby,
To pass the hours;
Send breezes through our trees!

You have a task
To carry out,
'Twas writ since time began,
The child must find
The father's home,
And thus become the man.

These journeys that
Primeval law
Established to occur,
Are fated ones.
Our destiny,
A passage, as it were.

The torch was passed
From hand to hand
In countries of the mind.
Yet emigrants,
On these shores come,
Forgot and left behind.

But not forgot
This blood-stirred place,
Where centuries had sped
The building up
Of families,
And then from which they'd fled.

Their journeys that
We distant know,
How fearful must have seemed.
Arrived on shore
At Ellis Isle,
They must have felt they dreamed.

And now you have
A pilgrimage
Reverse from those who came.
You're tracing them
To honor those
From whom you got your name.

So cat and I
Will keep the house,
And garden watered, too.
Until you come
From journeys far,
And we can welcome you!

- - - - - - - - - -

Pictures from Borzna

Synagogue in Borzna

View of Borzna River

House in Borzna

Original Borzna Shield

Modern Borzna Shield

Road leading to Borzna

Entrance to Borzna

Shapovalivka
(Where Borzna Jews were taken and shot by Nazis)

Borzna Houses

<><><><><><>

A lot has been written regarding the Holocaust. The account of the Jews here in Borzna is poignant and informative. I received an e-mail from another researcher interested in Borzna. While in Yad Vashem, Jerusalem, looking for a Yizkor book from Borzna (which he did not find), he ran across a letter from a woman school teacher who was another apparent eyewitness to what happened there. He transcribed this as follows:

A letter from a high school teacher from Borzna, Chernigovskoj County, Mrs. Semionowoj to Mr. J. M. Rosnovsky

October 31, 1995.

Dear Jakov Markovich!

Your letter arrived today, it was very exciting, I did not expect it. From time to time I was getting information about you. I'm very happy to get your letter, but you did not write anything about yourself and your family. Now here is the information you asked about.

The evacuation was very difficult. Bahmach [name of a town] was destroyed and bombed in July. All trucks left for the front and only a few horses were around. The evacuation started on 27th to the 30th of August—officially on 1st of September. A lot of people bought or got horses by September 5th to September 11th. The Army left Borzna and then at night, after a very short fight, the fascists entered the town. By this time a lot of people had not been evacuated. And soon many were also surrounded. Our dentist was one of them. She was killed and her husband.

More than 106-110 Jews were still left in Borzna. The situation was very difficult. Tenenbaum, kids, left. Old Tenenbaum stayed. It was exceptionally difficult for them. From day one fascists were mocking them. The soldiers were in Tenenbaum's house every day taking everything from them: cloth, utensils, buckets...Everybody was trying to help them with bread, metal cup, bucket...

Days and months were going by; it was very difficult to exist. Bad news came in from all sides—a lot of villages were burned to the ground. In the towns of Nezin, Chernigov, Konotop and others all of the Jewish population was killed.

Everybody was expecting something bad to happen.

The first to die was the humpbacked loader Chauskij. A policeman was walking him in a horse collar. He was sent to work, walked in a house and got shot. Jews were told to put on white armbands. Everybody was sent to work. We were cleaning barracks, dirt, and snow on the streets.

The first occurrence of a massacre of Jews was in January 1942. A bigshot from Kiev or Nezin came on January 18th. In the middle of the night all of the Jews were woken up by soldiers and police and sent to the village of Shapovalovka which is 10 km from Borzna. One-hundred and four Jews were shot there on the edge of an anti-tank ditch. Among them were old people, women, and children. Old man Urkin before the massacre was asked: "Do you want to live, old man?" He answered: "I'd like to know how all this will end." Misha said before dying that 'the enemies will pay for this with their blood.' Twenty-two year old Nina Krenhous died with her one year old daughter in her arms. A school teacher, Raisa Belaja, (daughter of bookbinder Baruch Belij) saw the massacre of her 16 year old son Misha and her sister Manja along with her children. The youngest was few months old. She was already in a confused state and did not understand anything except that all she worried about were her lost glasses.

Only a few escaped the massacre. Lisa Babkin ran away, but all her children were killed. She spent the rest of the occupation (2 years) in Konotop and is alive now. Three women who had Russian husbands escaped. The son of the hat maker Moisej Levin Yakov was hiding for more then a year but was found. Urkin was hiding in the hospital and escaped. Some Jews escaped massacres in their villages and were hiding with us. We were sending them to the guerilla fighters in Karijukowka. Only a few survived.

Now to Borzna came back all except the Miazorov's, Turowski's, and Strilazki's. In the summer of 1942 the army was going through day and night in the direction of the Volga river. And along with them thousands of Jewish men for work, but really they were walking to a slow death.

Moisej Levin's son, Abba committed suicide in 1941. His family is now living here.

Address: Rosnovsky J. M.
            Moscow 116
            Kasnokazarmennaja, 12 Corpus 4, apt. 23.[56]

Later, Alex Khatset, my Ukrainian friend who took me to Borzna, wrote that in his research in the Region Historical Archives he found no references to our family in Borzna. He was able to verify that the Germans occupied the town on September 11, 1941 and that it was liberated September 8, 1943. Also, during those two years, 126 people were killed while 179 were "removed" to Germany.

With so many stories about how the Ukrainians cooperated with the Nazis and of their anti-Semitism, it's refreshing to hear of those who saw a different side. I was reminded of this in a newspaper article commemorating the fiftieth anniversary of the liberation of Auschwitz. One regularly hears that the Russians freed the prisoners there. But this article reveals that it was a Ukrainian division that freed the camp from the retreating Germans on February 27, 1945. True,

---

[56] Jay D. Wall, Borzna, e-mail, 20 Jul 2000.

many prisoners remember how they treated the women brusquely and appeared to be unsympathetic. Yet one of them remembers the event in a more positive way. She reports that she was only an 11 year old girl when the Ukrainians came. Now 61, this woman recalls a soldier encountering her...

> *He picked me up and rocked me in his arms. Tears were flowing down his face. Somebody cared about me. I cannot forget that.*[57]

Even today, our souls can unite with that of a Ukrainian soldier.

In spite of all the difficulty, immigration across the Atlantic to America became one of the greatest movements of mankind. Between 1890 and 1930 almost 1,000,000 people entered the USA in the port of New York alone.

---

[57] Dean E. Murphy, *Jews Remember Horrors of Auschwitz; Poland: Hundreds meet on eve of liberation's anniversary. Their solemn gathering precedes official ceremonies*, Los Angeles Times—PART A, Friday, January 27, 1995.

CITIZENSHIP

Although my father will later have more to say about his father, now is a fitting time to relate the most recent discovery I was able to make concerning him. We have heard about how patriotic he was and how he felt about America. He owned a large American flag; he was inspired by marches and patriotic music; he wanted to participate and contribute to the American dream. My father said he early became an American citizen. When was that? How soon? I had recently read about the importance of finding naturalization papers, especially for the information that could be found in the original Declaration of Intent. But where could these be found? Where did he apply for citizenship; and when?

I was also interested in Motley. She would also have applied for citizenship. Before 1922, however, if the head of the household became naturalized, his accomplishment automatically included all the family members as well. So the date of Pesach's naturalization became especially important. Where this occurred was also significant since prior to 1906, naturalization papers were kept in the state where the application was made, and each court could handle naturalization any way it wished. After that everything was in Washington D.C.

Since this could have begun any time from 1904 on up, I thought I could get a clue if I could discover the year he registered to vote. Election years 1904, 1908, 1912, the family was living on La Crosse Street. Years 1916, 1920, etc., they were on Pine Street. I telephoned the election board in Madison, Wisconsin and in La Crosse. No records were kept that were that old. It was suggested I try the Clerk of the La Crosse County courts. I phoned her and said I was searching for the naturalization records for Peter Volkoff. She said that there were some old naturalization records kept there, and she would check for me. After a moment she came back and said, "We have records for a Pesach Volkoff. Would that be the same person?"

I could hardly wait for the mail to deliver this information. Holding the envelope from the La Crosse Court was a unique feeling. It was as though I was holding Pesach himself. Here were the answers. And, as usual, as I read and reread these documents, here were more questions. I tried to read as slowly and perceptibly as possible. There were obvious answers here, and then there were less obvious, hidden clues.

First, the index card, with everything neatly typed. The first shock—I have been misspelling his name. Not Pesach, but "Peysach." Maybe not the way we would normally spell that name today, but this is the way HE spelled his name, the way he signed his name. (And it wasn't just a misspelling on one page—it occurred each time the same way on all the documents.)

Then, the second shock—his birthday: Aug. 8, 1875. I had long ago found the month and year of his birth; now I knew the day, the eighth of August. And, guess what. His son (my father, Joe)—his first child to be born in America—was born on the eighth of August 1906! How did he do that?

His date of arrival in the United States, July 18, 1904, was not a surprise, but it is always nice to have documents that corroborate each other. And then, there it was—another nugget:

Date of naturalization
May 12, 1917

It took him almost 13 years. My father was ten years old—my Aunt Sally, 16. That is not "early" for me. Yet it shows remarkable perseverance. One wonders—was there a ceremony? Did the family go? Remember, not only Peysach, but Motley, Sarah, Rebecca, and Florence, all became American citizens on that day. You would think, considering the significance of this and the period of time it took to achieve this long-awaited and treasured goal, that the family would have gone to the ceremony or they would recall it, yet no one who was there remembers it. It is certainly a day of remembrance today for Peysach's descendants.

Then, another observation—**1917**. A year to be remembered in Russian history. The beginning of the Russian Revolution—serious disorders and riots in March, Czar Nicholas II abdicating the throne on March 17, power passing to Lenin and the Bolsheviks after the attack in November of the cruiser Aurora on Petrograd (Leningrad, St. Petersburg). If Peysach had waited a few more months to become a citizen, there wouldn't have been an Emperor of Russia to renounce.

Also here were the names of his friends—witnesses: Louis Nathenson, Sam Feinberg, Daniel

Family name	Given name or names
VOLKOFF	PEYSACH

Address: 1516 Pine St., La Crosse, Wisconsin
Certificate no. (or vol. and page): 698464 Vol. 3 P. 198 | Title and location of court: Circuit,La Crosse,Wis
Country of birth or allegiance: Russia | When born (or age): Aug. 8 1875
Date and port of arrival in U.S.: July 18, 1904 New York | Date of naturalization: May 12, 1917
Names and addresses of witnesses: Louis Nathenson, 612 No 9th St., Daniel Lenske, 423 Adams St.
U. S. Department of Justice, Immigration and Naturalization Service. Form N-85 (Old I-P)

Naturalization Index Card

Lensky. Marion recalled her cousin, Joe Lensky. Was Daniel Lensky his father? Was he the one who arrived first and met Peysach at Ellis Island? What a reunion that must have been.

All this from a 3x5 card!

Laying the card aside, another puzzle piece appears. It is a small paper with the title: **Circuit Court of the United States.** It says all the right things, such as when he arrived, and stating his intention to become a citizen of the United States, renouncing allegiance to the "Emperor of Russia." Looking carefully at the document, I noticed it said "FOR THE SOUTHERN DISTRICT OF NEW YORK." What was he doing in New York if he became a citizen while living in Wisconsin? And then I saw the date: November 26, 1904! Only four months after he had arrived from Ukraine, via England, he had filed an intention to become a citizen. This thought must have been in Peysach's mind when he arrived and was probably there even when he left. Why did it take 13 years? What was he doing in New York? How long did he stay there? When did he go to Wisconsin? What was Daniel Lensky's role in all this?

Peysach Volkoff's Declaration of Intent

The document was called a Declaration of Intent or more commonly, "First Papers". Although it doesn't contain a great deal of genealogical information of the "tombstone" variety, it tells a great deal about the thinking of Peysach and of the type of person he was. Naturalization was, for most immigrants, a long process. It most likely involved many classes learning to read, write, and speak English. It would also be necessary to learn about the history and process of American government. Because many immigrants either lacked great incentive or worked long hours, or both, citizenship was low on the list of priorities, and they were not likely to have applied to become citizens.

"First Papers" was filed in court as the application to begin to seek citizenship. It tells us that only four months after arrival, Peysach was intent on pursuing citizenship, and that somehow, for the next thirteen years (three Presidential elections), he didn't lose that goal. It almost is a more telling document than the citizenship papers themselves.

In addition to all this, it contains the following statement: Peysach Volkoff of 171 Clinton St City of NY. This was his first address (that we now know of) in the U.S. It is conveniently close to Ellis Island. It was probably a boarding house, maybe filled with Russian-Jewish immigrants. Was Daniel Lensky staying there? How long did he stay there before leaving for Wisconsin? What is there today? There is also the question of his family arriving in 1905. Did he meet them at Ellis Island? Did they all stay here before leaving for La Crosse? If not, perhaps he showed it to them: "Here was my first home in America."

The final document was the **Petition for Naturalization**. This document was filed once all the requirements for naturalization were satisfied. Although I don't know whether the actual certificate of naturalization still exits, it really is not too important, since it is simply a fancy paper with little interesting information. This Declaration, on the other hand, has a wealth of information on it. Almost all the information I had already obtained previously from other sources. The date of arrival, the ship name, the date and place of birth—all were known and this simply was additional verification.

Yet one fragment jumped out. We have always celebrated Aunt Sally's birthday on July fourth. No one knew the year for sure, and even the day was suspect. July fourth seemed as appropriate as any other date. Immigrants have been known to take that date as the date they came to America or as an important date in their lives. She herself has said she just always remembered celebrating her birthday on the Fourth of July but wasn't sure that really was her birth day. She also wasn't certain of the year. Now here was her father saying on a vital document that the birthday of his first child was July 4, 1901. This is the next best thing to a birth certificate, which no doubt doesn't exist. Who else would know the birth date of his first child? Thirteen years after arriving there would be no incentive to lie. And on a document as important to him as this one was, he wouldn't want to do anything but be truthful.

Yet, there is still something that perpetuates the mystery. A small "(15)" is inscribed next to the birth date. Why? It would have been her age at the time of the document. It wasn't done for any of the other five children. Perhaps he only knew her age, not the exact date. Did they decide at the time to use July 4th, the Clerk of the Court filling out the form leaving the "(15)" as a clue that the age was correct, the date was made-up?

Or perhaps, this wasn't so strange at that time for them. Many people born in Europe in the 1800's or early in this century and some born in the U.S. during that same period did not know their exact dates of birth, and their children may not have known even what they knew. But it probably never mattered much to them either.

Petition for Naturalization - Front

IN THE MATTER OF THE PETITION OF

OATH OF ALLEGIANCE

I hereby declare, on oath, that I absolutely and entirely renounce and abjure all allegiance and fidelity to any foreign prince, potentate, state, or sovereignty, and particularly to The present Government *of* Russia *of whom I have heretofore been a subject and that I further renounce the title of* _____ *or order of nobility, which I have heretofore held; that I will support and defend the Constitution and laws of the United States of America against all enemies, foreign and domestic; and that I will bear true faith and allegiance to the same.*

Subscribed and sworn to before me, in open Court, this ____ day of May A. D. 1917.

ORDER OF COURT ADMITTING PETITIONER

ORDER OF COURT DENYING PETITION

THE SAID PETITION IS HEREBY DENIED.

MEMORANDUM OF CONTINUANCES

REASONS FOR CONTINUANCE

Continued from _____ 19__
to _____ 19__
Continued from _____ 19__
to _____ 19__

NAMES OF SUBSTITUTED WITNESSES

Certificate of Naturalization No. 628464 issued on the 12th day of May A. D. 1917.

Petition for Naturalization - reverse

—— LIFE IN NEW YORK ——

The Petition finally yields one last bit of information that, of course, raises further questions. It states that Peysach resided in the United States of America for the required five years since arriving in 1904. It also states that he has lived in the state of Wisconsin for at least one year preceding the date of the Petition, and that he has lived in Wisconsin since March 1, 1905. That means he must have lived in New York for about nine months before going to Wisconsin; he didn't leave immediately. It makes sense now that the Intention to file for Citizenship was completed four months after arriving in New York. Did he stay at the Clinton Street address for that time? What did he do; what was his job?

Once again, Simche's experience gives us food for thought. On the boat he had made friends with a total stranger, an American who traveled often to Europe. At the dock this man introduced him to a Mr. Averbach and was told that he would take care of him. Actually, I think Daniel Lensky knew that Peysach was arriving and met him there. Perhaps what happened to Simche was similar to what happened to Peysach. Instead of Mr. Averbach, he was met by Daniel Lensky, a relative.

> Mr. Averbach was a *lantzman*, a fellow countryman. He and his wife were both from Warshilovka, the same town that Simche came from. They had been in New York many years…. They had a wine cellar on Orchard Street…They wanted to see someone from Warshilovka. So they were watching reports on immigrants and where they were coming from. And all of a sudden they got a letter from the rabbi in Warshilovka, informing them that Simche Charnofsky was on the way to New York on the boat *St. Louis,* and begging them to do what they could for him.[58]

It was on this same boat that Peysach arrived one year later. Orchard Street is not far from Clinton Street. Do you suppose Peysach would have purchased a bottle of wine at times from them?

---

[58] Charnofsky, op.cit., p.224.

So the Averbachs decided first to meet him at the boat…[to bring him to his first dinner]. To try to get some kind of a job for him—to establish him and help him as much as they could.

And what a reception he had when he arrived! Mrs. Averbach kissed him as if he were her own brother…everybody was concerned with Simche, asking questions about Warshilovka, about the people who lived there, about some of their relatives…This went on into the late hours, when…Mr. Averbach showed Simche to his room next door, which they rented for him and had paid three dollars for room and board for the first week.

The next day…they discussed what he could do. He was not a tailor, not a painter, not a worker at all. Simche's family…were all merchants. And it was decided that Simche should become a pushcart peddler. They showed him where to get a pushcart, and where he could buy apples, pears, or other fruit. Simche became a businessman.

Every day he pushed his cart on Esther or Orchard Street, selling apples, pears, plums, and other fruit…When he sold out he called it a day…And sometimes they were long hours—ten, twelve, and fourteen, for he had to sell everything—he counted a dollar profit. Working five days a week, he had five dollars a week.[59]

Peysach, too, was not a worker. The memory is that the Volkovitskys operated a feed store in Borzna. Did he, too, become a peddler?

Simche decided to send home a dollar a week to Molke. This didn't leave much to survive on. He got another job as a night watchman in a clothing shop on Forsythe Street. There was no salary but he could sleep on the cutting table and eat breakfast and dinner there. He would sweep up the swatches and waste cloth into bags and sell it to a ragman for three to five dollars a week. This was Simche's lodging place

---

[59] Ibid., p.225.

What made Peysach decide to go to Wisconsin? To La Crosse? After all, he could have been a "junk dealer" anywhere.

Then, three months after arriving in La Crosse, Martha arrived on the twenty-ninth of May with their three daughters. Did he go back to New York to greet the arriving family? He must have.

All this is all we know of the father and mother that came from Ukraine. Dimitri Yurasov was cataloging Stalin's purges. Looking for the history of his father, one person wrote,

> In his catalog, Dima found my father's name. He named the place of his imprisonment and, evidently, his death. Dima showed me that…my father was a librarian. Was this some arbitrary thing he did in the camps or his real profession, I don't know. But something changed inside me. From the anonymous gray mass of pea jackets, my father had emerged as a particular man, a special man. Not all were called librarians! A father! I have a father! [60]

---

[60] pg.31

FUTURE WORK

A number of questions remain about this family some of which are posited in this account. If one waits for all the questions to be answered the "painting" is never finished. So even when the questions remain unanswered the questions are presented here and the current knowledge is shared. Future answers await future family historians. Developments in the computer field will make research easier as documents which now are unavailable become easier to access. In addition, errors that others may discover herein may be corrected.

Also, interests may be stimulated by reading one of the items listed at the end of this book in the bibliography. Some of these references provide further information that may interest the reader.

This work provides the first steps, and inquiring minds will continue to add to this work. The Volkoffs and their friends will not now be forgotten, and the soil for future historians is prepared—welcome to this exciting and rewarding work!

MY LIFE: AN AUTOBIOGRAPHY

By
Joe DuVal (Volkoff)

- - - - - - - - - -

Towards the end of my father's life, he wrote his autobiography. He was blind then and used a typewriter to externalize the experiences he remembered. When I discovered it years later, I used it to begin the genealogical research herein presented. But more important than that, it gave me an insight into a world that had disappeared and would have been irretrievable had these experiences not been written down. It doesn't make the present (or future) any better or worse, but it gives a depth to one's experience and provides a background one wishes were there in previous generations. It gives not only a background for a specific family but provides an insight into a special historical period in the Midwest, what it was like to grow up in an immigrant family during the early part of the twentieth century.

The words are his. Major grammatical or spelling errors were corrected, but generally the structure is as it was in the original text. Typing it into a computer has to have been easier to do for me than was his originally typing it blind on a typewriter! Occasionally I have inserted information, e.g. e-mail that is germane to what he has typed or memories of a family member that contributes to his thoughts.

- - - - - - - - - -

MY FAMILY

My father never played fiddle for the Czar, but he did play the clarinet in the Czar's army band just after the turn of the century; that is, until he went AWOL with the Russo-Japanese War brewing. He headed for the United States of America and kept going until he was halfway across that broad land, where he settled down in the bustling little lumber town of La Crosse, Wisconsin, population about 25,000. Here he was joined a year later by my mother and her three small daughters, and here, on August 8, 1906, I, Joseph Volkoff, first saw the light of day. (The DuVal cognomen came twenty-six years later, in 1932, but that's getting ahead of my story.) Here, too, my two younger sisters were born, and dad and mother wound up with a family of one son and five daughters.

Dad was a hard working, fun loving, God fearing man with a passionate love for his family. He was a pious Orthodox Jew who would not so much as strike a match to kindle a fire on the Sabbath.

When dad first disembarked at Ellis Island, one of the officials called, "Hey, Pete, come over here." So he immediately adopted the name Peter, which he kept for the duration of his life. Had he but known that Peter was the foremost disciple of Jesus, I'm sure he would not have been in such a hurry to take the name as his own.

[There has been quite a correspondence in the Jewishgen discussion group regarding name changes. I don't know if my father's account is true or not, but, apparently, this is the story he was told, and it sounds reasonable. At least the name wasn't changed by an official, but, according to this account, the "adoption" of Pete was a self-implemented modification.]

I'd like to add to what Mr. Lapin wrote. I know of stories where Jews in order to leave Russia and avoid military conscription took someone else's papers, generally someone in the family who was much younger. Once they got to the U.S. or elsewhere, the name on the papers became their given name. Thus a Salomon may have become Jacob, or a Jacob may have become a Solomon, and so on down the line. Then to complicate matters, the Immigration Officials made mincemeat of family names. I have a friend who claims that a friend of his is called Weissnicht. The story is that at Ellis Island, when the immigration official asked a question, the old man's response "Weiss Nicht," meaning "I do not know" in Yiddish and that became the American name of the family. One of the oldest jokes in this matter is the

Jew whose name is Shane Fergusson. That was so because he indicated that he had already forgotten something, or these words in Yiddish. The joke is probably apocryphal but as we know, jokes always have an element of truth in them.

Avrum Lapin wrote:

> *Then there was my Uncle Frank (nee Chiam) who arrived in Canada at the age of 13 (which his parents and 7 siblings). So the story goes when he went to School in Canada he was asked his name and he said Chiam and the teacher replied, "I shall call you Frank". And he became Frank (his mother's passport and the ship's manifest both say Chiam). His younger brother, Itzhak on the passport, became Sam in Canada perhaps to pave his way into Medical School.*[61]

[Another person wrote this and although it may be generally true, we don't need to disregard other experiences:]

> The writer must be new to Jewish Genealogy because the first thing we all learn is: Names were not changed at Ellis Island (unless, in rare circumstances, when they were "corrected" on the ship manifest/immigration record) and immigration officials did NOT change anyone's surname or ask an immigrant his name for the purpose of "transliterating it." Please read Warren Blatt's FAQ and the infofiles in JewishGen. It's bad enough when non-genealogists perpetuate this myth and we have to convince them otherwise. Long ago, my father told me the "Shane Furgusson" joke and STILL doesn't fully believe the truth because he has heard everybody else tell the same stupid joke.[62]

[Lastly, this seems likely as to what really happened there.]

[61] Marc Raizman, the Name Changes, e-mail, 19 Jun 1999.
[62] Mark Nearenberg, Esq., e-mail, New York, NY.

It might help to have myths about name changes on Ellis Island disappear if people knew why they were not true. Some of you have seen the Documentary "Ellis Island" on the History Channel or A&E with Mandy Potenkin. I was hired to do the document research for the series, and I was one of the six "talking heads" who took the viewer on a tour of the Island. We spent more than one of the three hours discussing this name change and similar problems and myths.

1) The system was designed so that if a person had no medical or legal issues they would get on and off the Island without generating a single sheet of paper. Detainees, for example, created a "paper event" because as a result of being detained, they "generated" Form 215. People not detained with a (few rare exceptions) were only to be found on the manifest itself. The manifests were created mostly at the ports of embarkation with the occasional change made aboard ship.

2) Officials from the Bureau of Immigration (BOI) were not permitted to write words on the manifests! They were only permitted to put check marks in appropriate places. (Yes there are some exceptions but the exception makes the rule.)

3) Seeing thousands of people a day, the last thing they had to do was think up names for people.

4) There is absolutely no documentary evidence of name changes. Supervisors were permitted to write in pencil (sometimes they "cheated" with pens) when an immigrant complained personally about the incorrect spelling of a name and requested that it be changed.

What really happened—a person would be called up to the standing desk and the BOI officials would mispronounce their name. Some, who were in awe and fear of the process, independently decided that this was their new name in America.

There is anecdotal evidence that relatives who came to get their "Greener" relations would request that the name appear a certain way on the manifest to avoid problems and inconsistencies later on. Name changes occurred later on when people applied for jobs, went to school, got drafted, etc.[63]

[A recent book contained the information about a practice regarding the naming of sons in Czarist Russia. Under the laws at that time, a son was excused from military service if he was an 'only son'. Therefore, some Jewish families would list sons, after the first, with different parents—different family names. This way, they could avoid service.][64]

Oddly enough, one of my sisters who had been named Rebecca, had early in life, picked up the name Mary, by which she was known most of her life—she now carries the more graceful appellation of Marion. So here we have the curious paradox of a strictly orthodox Jewish family, one member of which was named after a disciple of Jesus, the other after the mother of Jesus. Speaking of names, Dad's last name was originally Volkovitsky, which he shortened to Volkoff upon reaching America, a practice of many immigrants of the early twentieth century. To support his growing family, Dad worked hard as a junk dealer, buying and selling old rags, paper, and metals. Physically, he was a handsome man, short of stature (just a bit over five feet tall), with a tendency toward plumpness—a tribute to mother's cooking abilities.

Americanization did not come easily to him. He was very proud of the fact that he early became an American citizen. He had a hard time mastering the English language, and spoke with a decided accent, much more so than mother. Both mother and dad insisted on their children talking English to them, and they did their best to answer in kind, which is probably one reason why the only Russian words I can remember are "borscht" and "perozshna". When dad got angry, instead of cussing American style, he would yell, "Hoochis, croochis, tah-pah-yay!" I always felt pretty sure this meant something very bad in Russian, although I was never able to verify it.

63 Rafi Guber, <u>Ellis Island: It might help to know why the myth is a myth,</u> 21 Jun 1999
64 Yaffa Eliach, *There Once Was A World;A 900 Year Chronicle Of The Shtetl Of Eishyshok*, p.

In trying to Americanize my father, whom we always called "Pa" (and since all my friends called their father "Dad"), I once brazenly said, "Dad,…" Well, all hell broke loose. I was frightened and was frozen to the floor, as with his decided accent he shouted, "Dead! I am not dead yet!" From then on, it was ALWAYS "Pa". I can laugh about it now, but at the time this episode was deadly serious.

My "Pa" was proudly patriotic. He would stand at attention anytime the National Anthem was played. He bought and displayed the largest American flag over our house every Fourth of July.

Reminiscence of Betty (Volkoff) Marks, 8/91

Mother was a true pioneer-type woman. She would have fitted in well in the old covered wagon days when the women helped their men blaze a trail through the western wilderness. Alone and unaided she made the trip from Russia to the United States in the steerage compartment of a great oceangoing vessel, with her three young daughters, one an infant in her arms. She was a proud, courageous woman, slight of build, but a fighter from the word "go". I remember once, when one of the school bullies dirtied our front porch by throwing horse manure on it, she caught him, took away his cap, and didn't return it until he had cleaned up every vestige of the mess he had caused. She lived a hard life: cooking, baking, sewing, scrubbing, washing, working endlessly for her beloved brood of six children and her husband. Long after everyone had gone to bed, she would sit at her sewing machine making dresses for her daughters so they could go to school neat and well clothed. Mother was also a very religious person, keeping two sets of dishes, one for dairy foods, one for meat dishes, and, of course, a third set which was used only during the Passover week. Every Friday evening she lit the Sabbath candles, and she believed implicitly in the power of God to help us through all our difficulties. Mother was made of stern fiber and nothing dismayed her. She was the stronger character of the two. When the occasion demanded corporal punishment, it was mother, not dad, who did the administering. Mother outlived dad by about eleven years, and even then she was too proud to live with one of her daughters. She felt that she did not want to be a burden to them and preferred living by herself. When her grandchildren came, she would visit her daughters and help with the babies, but as soon as she felt that her help was no longer needed, back she would go to her apartments in Ocean Park, California.

I just learned from Marion that Joe Lensky, our cousin, told her that my mother, as a young girl in Russia, was so attractive that people would turn around to look at her when she walked down the street. I also recall thinking how beautiful she looked at High Holy Days in our little schul in La Crosse.

Reminiscence of Betty (Volkoff) Marks, 8/91

I never had a feeling of real closeness to either of my parents. Part of this was my own fault, as I was not a confiding child, preferring to work out my problems by myself. I feel that dad would have liked to have been closer to me, but didn't quite know how to go about it. He was of the Old World, and it was hard for him to understand the interests and problems of a growing American boy. I was a southpaw, and it used to make him very angry when I would use my left hand to hold an axe while chopping wood. He felt it was somehow abnormal. Dad also showed a pathetic eagerness to conform to American tastes while I was going to high school; he would invariably choose one of my flashiest ties to wear in preference to his own conservative ones.

> *My father was a very intelligent man who took great delight in helping me figure my arithmetic problems in the sixth grade—he would figure out the answer in such a roundabout way. When I was the only one in the class who had the correct answer, and when the teacher, who was also the principal, asked if anyone had helped me, I assured him that I figured it out all by myself. Why was I ashamed to tell him that my father had figured out the entire problem?*

Reminiscence of Betty (Volkoff) Marks, 8/91

Mother, on the other hand, made little effort to understand me or my problems. She, of course, had five daughters to care for, and having once been a little girl herself, could better cope with the problems of little girls than of a little boy. She never knew how deeply she hurt me when, as a boy of about ten or eleven, I brought her a huge beautiful bouquet of wild flowers which I had picked especially for her back in the bluffs and coulees which lay in the eastern boundaries of our city. Instead of even pretending that she liked them, her reaction was to scold me for tearing my shirt on some brambles and for getting my face dirty. With hot tears of disappointment welling up in my eyes because of her lack of appreciation for what I considered a beautiful bouquet, I would woefully take the flowers to either Mrs. Lansing or Mrs. Shaeffer, our next-door neighbors, who would receive them with effusive enthusiasm.

> (ED: My father would have probably understood this better if he had been more familiar with Jewish tradition. Perhaps this is best expressed in a book I recently read. The first two chapters tell of his relationship with his parents and is worth looking at if only for that reason. It especially notes how the author wished to have the same approval his mother gave to his sisters. "I was hoping that my mother would treat me the way she treated my sisters...but her religious convictions demanded that she regard me as a man. From the time I turned five

years old, she was not supposed to touch me…I was not caressed by either of my parents."[65]

In later years, when I thought a little brunet from Memphis, Tennessee had broken my heart (although I later decided she had just wounded my pride), my first thought was to rush back to mother and pour out my heart to her. I felt sure she would understand, but she didn't. I felt no sympathy or understanding, although she didn't say so in so many words. I sensed that she felt I was showing weakness of which she disapproved. My sister, Florence, who had a much better understanding of the situation, introduced me to an attractive girl friend of hers, and with the help of my brother-in-law's car, it wasn't long before I had forgotten the fickle little gal from Dixie.

Years later, when I first became interested in Christian Science, I again felt certain that mother would understand my interest if given the chance. Again I was wrong. To mother, a Christian is a Christian and a Jew is a Jew, and anybody who left Judaism for any form of Christianity was a traitor. She was sure that I would be worshipping Jesus as God, that our home would be filled with crucifixes, and nothing could convince her I wasn't lying when I told her she was wrong. She insisted I talk to a rabbi about it, which I did to please her, but here she made a mistake. The gentleman in question was far removed from what my idea of a spiritual leader should be. I visited him at his home which was disheveled, the harmony of which was disturbed by the squalling of several untidy looking children. He, himself, a bit on the paunchy side, was wearing a vest upon which clung bits of dried food. His eyes looked harassed, frustrated, holding none of the calm serenity and peace of mind which to me is such a necessary adjunct of a spiritual leader. Probably well coached by my mother, I could tell at once he was completely ignorant of the basic fundamentals of Christian Science; I could have asked him about the teachings of Buddha or Zoroaster and would have received the same answer. My dream of a logical, intelligent discussion of the problem was soon dissipated, and as soon as I was able I pressed a five dollar bill into his palm and quickly departed. Let me state here that I do not consider him an example of

---

65 Maurice Shainberg, *Breaking from the KGB*, p.13.

the average rabbi. I have known a number of rabbis, Orthodox and Reformed, who were intelligent and well qualified, both mentally and morally, to be able leaders of their flocks. But to get back to my family…

Our family was a closely knit group in those early days of my growing-up period. Unhampered by the disconcerting effects of radio, of television, of convertible coupes and other forms of high speed motor cars, with the silent flickers still a toy to be enjoyed of a Saturday afternoon for a nickel or a dime, we were forced to entertain ourselves. Many a long winter evening was spent in playing favorite parlor games such as Twenty Questions and Animal-Vegetable-Mineral. There was always a deck of cards handy for a session of Hearts, Whist, or Casino, and although we seldom bought a book, we did a land-office business at the public library.

Although lunch was usually a hit-or-miss affair, eaten singly or in pairs (as we rushed home from school during the noon hour), dinner was almost always a complete family get-together, lively, noisy, sometimes boisterous, as we recounted the experiences of the day. Dad sat beaming at the head of the table, while mother, her face flushed from close contact with the hot wood-burning stove, did most of the serving.

My sisters and I always got along well. There has never been any serious trouble between them and me, or between the girls themselves. Oh, I remember once when Rose ran crying out of the room when I teased her about some boy friend or other, but never has there been any serious feuds. Now that we are all pretty well scattered, there are times when I do not hear from one or more of my sisters for a year or more. But nobody resents this. When we do write, our letters are always welcomed and we excuse our lack of frequent writing as a family trait of which we are all guilty.

Sally always impressed me as the most serious of my five sisters. As she was the firstborn, she felt a responsibility towards the rest of the family which many times involved self-sacrifice on her part and she gave of herself unstintingly. Even with the family grown, when dad needed help in his grocery business in Minneapolis, and I didn't seem to fit in, she gave up a good secretarial job in order to devote her whole time to helping the family business.

When I think back to my sister Marion in her teens, I recall a pretty girl full of irrepressible gaiety, combined with a sharp temper. I can see her now at the dinner table, laughing until the tears streamed down her cheeks, as she recounted some hilarious experience of the day. When she was aroused at any misdeed of mine, real or fancied, I learned early to stay out of her way until the storm had subsided, which usually didn't take too long as her temper cooled as quickly as it flared up.

My sister Florence, the babe-in-arms my mother brought with her from Russia, was considered the bright one of the family. She was known as the "goote kepele", the good little head, and she it was who entered high school at the tender age of twelve and, upon graduation, was selected as the valedictorian of her class. How proud we were of her as she stepped to the platform and delivered a zealous oration on child labor, one of the burning issues of the day.

Rosalie was aptly named, for her outstanding characteristic was a friendly, smiling, cheerful, "rosy" disposition. She radiated happiness and harmony, seemed to like everybody, and was loved by all in return.

Far be it from me to upset the harmonious relationships which now exist between me and my sisters by attempting to name one as my favorite. Suffice it to say that at various periods of my life each has occupied that place in my heart. As the baby of the family, Boots has always been the family favorite. She was the athlete of the family, city tennis champion at seventeen, adept at softball, supple of body and swift of foot, yet, withal, maintaining her feminine charm and grace.

> *Joe taught me a number of things. I loved to play baseball with the boys on the corner lot. Joe taught me how to catch a ball—how to hold on to it— that helped me to make first team baseball throughout my entire college years. I was a excellent catcher, but the world's <u>worst</u> batter!*
>
> *When I was ten years old, Joe Bregman, a cousin from Minneapolis, was visiting us in La Crosse, and brought Joe a chess set. Joe studied it thoroughly, taught me the game, and we were forever avid players. I, in turn, taught Marty and our two sons, and we would have hot family tournaments.*
>
> Reminiscence of Betty (Volkoff) Marks, 8/91

So much for the Volkoff sisters, each of whom I'm sure could write far more authentically of her own experiences than can I. As far as my family tree is concerned, I'm afraid I can't go back very far. My grandparents on both mother's and father's side never did get out of Russia. We lost track of them years ago and must presume they have now passed on.

Early Impressions
(Age…3-5)

Directly across the street from our home at 1614 La Crosse Street was the Oak Grove Cemetery. I was fascinated by the funeral processions—the somber, black hearse leading the way, drawn usually by a pair of spirited coal black stallions, followed by the horse drawn carriages containing the mourners. My sisters and I would perch on the fence which surrounded the cemetery in round-eyed (sic) wonder as the funeral services were conducted, and if we were lucky we would witness the dramatic sight of a weeping bereaved one attempting to throw herself into the grave. Then, after the funeral party left, we would approach the new grave site to admire the beautiful floral wreaths.

The streetcar tracks ran right past our home on La Crosse Street, and it was one of our greatest delights to sit on the curb facing the tracks, drinking our "taelle mit meelchele" (tea and milk), munching on our homemade cookies, and watching the streetcars go by. During the summer months we loved to watch the unenclosed "summer cars" as they carried gaily dressed men and women to the nearby baseball park. Occasionally an automobile of the "one lunger" variety would putt-putt-putt by, but our greatest thrill was to watch runaway horses, a fairly common sight, as they careened madly down the street, dragging a wagon or carriage behind them.

The first doctor I can remember, Dr. Wolff, was a perfect example of a typical small town general practitioner. He not only looked like a doctor, with his Van Dyke goatee, but he smelled mysteriously of liniment, medicines, and peppermint lozenges. A rather stout man with round rosy cheeks and a cheerful bedside manner, I can remember his winter visits best, for he always came in a horse drawn sleigh, and his arrival was announced by the merry jingle of his sleigh bells. He would enter, a big bear of a man, wearing a fur coat, satchel in hand, to attend our runny noses and sore throats. Later, I went to school with his two sons who were just as rosy cheeked as he was.

The only other physician of my childhood with whom I came in contact besides Dr. Wolff was a Dr. Evans, a trim, not at all doctorish-looking man, clean-shaven, with friendly, piercing grey eyes. My parents had taken me to him as a last resort to cure a case of bed-wetting. Whippings, threats of being sent to reform school, and being sent to bed without my supper had proved of no avail. Dr. Evans wisely told me that he himself had suffered with the same affliction as a boy. He gave me some blue pills which fascinated me, for they caused my urine to turn blue, but which had absolutely no effect on the basic problem—I eventually grew out of it. I still remember Dr. Evan's advice on how to stay healthy: "Always walk on the balls of your feet, never with any weight on your heels, and walk with your feet turned slightly inward, as the Indians do, and you'll never get sick." I probably should have taken this advice more seriously.

If curiosity is really an indication of intelligence, I must have been a very intelligent little boy, for I was forever delving into the why and wherefore of things. Once I wondered what a frost covered iron fence would taste like. Luckily, I tested with just the tip of my tongue, or I would have really been riveted to that fence. As it was, I was able to tear myself away with only a burning feeling to pay for my folly. Another time, I almost burned down our home when I was curious as to whether or not a celluloid comb would burn. It was a Friday evening, just after mother had lit the Sabbath candles. She had placed a candle in her bedroom. I wandered in a few moments later, saw the candle on the dresser with the comb beside it, and decided to find the answer to the question, "Would a comb burn?" I quickly found the answer to be affirmative. With a howl I dropped the flaming comb on the dresser and ran for help. Luckily, mother had been drying some dishes and was in the kitchen with a towel in her hands. She rushed to the bedroom, smothered the flames (which had already begun to make some headway), and saved our home.

When I was about four years old I was standing by an open window one day about the noon hour with my little hands on the window sill, when wham! down came the window frame, pinning my fingers between the frame and the sill, and holding them there as in a vice. I yelled and pulled and stomped my feet, all to no avail—I just couldn't free myself. Mother tried to raise the window, but my fingers were wedged in so tightly she could not budge it. In desperation she ran next door to our neighbors, the Felts, and luckily for me, Mr. Felt was home for lunch. He rushed over, raised the window frame, and I gratefully removed my pinched fingers. Fortunately, no bones were broken, and I was more scared than hurt. From then on I was very wary of window sills.

One wintry morning during my preschool days, one of my sisters took me for a walk past the Washington School which she attended. By the side of the red brick building lay a huge pile of firewood. She pointed to the building and said, "That's my school." Somehow or other, I thought she was pointing at the pile of wood, and for months thereafter the word school to me was synonymous with a huge pile of wood. It was confusing to me, when my sisters left for school each morning, to understand why it was so important for them to go visit a pile of wood every day.

My kindergarten days are rather hazy in my memory, but they must have been pleasant enough. I remember cutting out paper figures with a blunt edged pair of scissors, of using a paste pot, of marching and dancing around the room to the music of a piano. I even remember my teacher's name—Miss Sabowitz—which is more than I can say of a lot of my high school teachers.

One bright May afternoon I was on my way home from kindergarten when I was intercepted by one of my sisters who told me that I couldn't go home yet since the stork was visiting my mother, and before he left I was to have a new little brother or sister. This stork business confused me, as mother had told me that when I was born she had stood outside the door, God had thrown me down from heaven, and she had caught me in her apron. Be it stork or be it apron, when I did get home, I had a little red-faced baby sister, Bertha, or Boots as she was soon to be known.

Two things stand out in my memory of Boots as a baby. First, the way she would point at our house cat and say, "Tllll, Tllll," the first word she ever spoke. Then, there was her mode of locomotion before she was able to walk. Instead of crawling around on all fours as do most children, she would sit upright with her legs outstretched, then, drawing her legs in, she would hunch her bottom forward, then repeat the process again and again. She really got around.

- - - - - - - - - -

From the 1910 Census

Baking Day
1912-1913
(Age 6-7)

What is the most delectable tidbit that ever delighted your taste buds? A savory, sizzling steak, perhaps? Or maybe a helping of tender southern fried chicken done to a crisp, golden brown? Delicious as these may be, none can compare in hunger-appeasing satisfaction to a growing boy with the taste-tempting goodness of a slice of hot, steaming, homemade bread just out of the oven with its flavor enhanced by generous chunks of yellow butter, topped with homemade strawberry jam. What a mouth watering gob of goo!

Except in rare cases, children today are cheated out of this appetizing experience. Store-bought bread cannot begin to compare in taste with the home baked variety. Friday was baking day in our little home, and each Friday we would hurry home from school so as to be there when mother pulled the brown, delicious smelling loaves out of the oven. She would bake enough bread to last us a week; several loaves of rye, several loaves of white, and always there was one large white loaf of "challah", the braided loaf that was placed at the head of the table each Friday night to grace the Sabbath meal. With bits of dough left over on purpose, mother would make what she called "flageles", little birds, which, by deft twisting and kneading, actually looked like little birds, with a head, wings, tail, and even a pair of feet. Besides the bread, she would bake pastry goodies; cookies, cakes, perozshna, a jellied Russian-type cake, and, during the Purim festival, she would make "hamen tashen", a mouth melting tart with a simply scrumptious honeyed poppyseed filling. Another delicacy mother would often concoct was a sort of meat pie she called "bobka" with a ground meat filling called "loongen" which I presume was lung. It was indeed delicious.

Although we were a poor family in those days, there never seemed to be a lack of food in the house. There was always a barrel of apples in the cellar, and the shelves of the basement walls were filled with mason jars bearing canned vegetables and fruits of every description. We always had a yard full of chickens which provided eggs and meat. Fish were both plentiful and cheap, and there was always a huge potful of stew or chicken soup simmering on the kitchen stove. Each year dad would borrow a cabbage cutter and cut up enough cabbages to make a barrel of sauerkraut, enough to last us a year. In this barrel, besides the kraut would go a couple of small watermelons, some tomatoes, green apples, and pepper plants. I'll never forget one of mother's specials—buckwheat cakes served with rich, fatty gravy made from roast chicken. Yes, we really ate well in those days, and for a combination food and medicine, our sore throats were always eased by a glass of "goggle-moggle", a hot eggnog which always hit the spot. And I mustn't forget those annual spring trips to Myrick Park in which the entire family participated in picking dandelion flowers until we had several baskets full. Dad would make some wonderfully tasting dandelion wine, and mother would make a jam or jelly out of what remained. Yes, those were happy days.

First Grades
1912-13
(Age 6-7)

It's peculiar how names and personalities of some of our teachers remain etched in our memories, while those of others just completely disappear. I'll never forget Miss Becker, my first grade teacher, probably because she had a stroke earlier in life and carried her head at an angle. On the other hand, I can't bring to mind either the name or the features of my second grade teacher, although I do remember learning the alphabet there—and simple addition.

The Christmas season was not a happy one for me as a child. Mother had forbidden us to join in the singing of Christmas carols, and while the other children were caroling their praise of "the little Lord Jesus", I would sit there unhappily with my lips tightly pressed together. Miss Becker had once asked me why I didn't join in the singing. When I told her my parents wouldn't allow me to, she said, "Oh, fiddle! They're beautiful songs, and there's no reason why you shouldn't enjoy them along with the rest of us." I just sat there miserably and closed my lips tighter than ever.

I did love the Christmas trees of the period, though—the old-fashioned ones one seldom sees these days, festooned with popcorn balls, apples, and crinkly Christmas candy. Those were the days before electric lighting of the trees, and it's a miracle there weren't a lot more tragic fires than actually occurred, caused by the open candle lighting of the trees.

Speaking of electric lights, I must have been nine or ten years old before we enjoyed electric lighting in our home. We used kerosene lamps and candles. I vividly remember cleaning the lamp chimneys of soot and trimming the wicks almost daily. Dad once averted what could well have been a tragedy when a burning wick slipped through the teeth which held it and fell into the bowl of the lamp containing the kerosene. The kerosene ignited and the whole bowl of the lamp was aflame. With rare presence of mind he picked up the lamp by the stem underneath the bowl, calmly opened the back door, and hurled the lamp into a snowbank in the yard where it burned out harmlessly. Why the kerosene didn't explode or why the glass bowl didn't crack and break up from the intense heat is a mystery to me. I suppose it was just another example of how God again had His arms around us in a moment of crisis.

THE RUBBER HOSE

Although my behavior as an elementary school boy was, for the most part, exemplary, and my deportment grades were consistently high, there were two occasions upon which I felt the smarting sting of the principal's rubber hose across the back of my trousers.

Our fourth-grade spelling book was made up of coarse, pulpy paper which I found out quite by accident had the absorbing qualities of a piece of blotting paper. I had spilled a drop of ink on one of the pages and was surprised to see how readily the ink was soaked up by the paper. Thereafter, I would get a morbid satisfaction out of dipping my pen in the inkwell, and then letting a blob of ink fall on one of the pages of the spelling book, watching with fascination as it spread and was absorbed. Before the semester was half over, almost every page in the book was full of ink splotches, in many cases completely obliterating words we were supposed to study. One day, my fourth-grade teacher caught a glimpse of one of these pages, and gasped in horror as she leafed through the book and saw what happened. She had me march right up to Mr. Hardy in the principal's office, book in hand, and explain to him what had happened.

Mr. Hardy, a venerable old Civil War veteran in his seventies, with a white, curly beard which made him look for all the world like the confederate hero, General Robert E. Lee, took a dim view of the situation. He reached for the rubber hose hanging from a peg on the wall, (despite his seventy-odd years he had lost none of the strength in his arm) and made me feel quite smartly the error of my ways.

Incidentally, Mr. Hardy retired the following year to spend his reclining (sic) years in Southern California, from whence we received amazing and unbelievable letters telling of roses blooming in his backyard during the Christmas season, and of geraniums growing in profusion, whereas geraniums in Wisconsin could be found only as potted plants.

Mr. Kircher, his successor, was a younger man, very prim and proper-looking, reminding me, in retrospect, of a young Woodrow Wilson. He had a chance to try out the rubber hose on me when I was in the fifth-grade. It happened one windy afternoon just as the recess bell was ringing to call us back to our classes. The outside doors to the schoolhouse were being held wide-open to allow us to hurry inside. The playground adjoining the school was composed of a combination of sand and crushed cinders. I noticed that if I scuffed my feet, a cloud of dust arose which was carried off in swirling eddies by the wind. The harder I scuffed, the greater the cloud of dust which arose. I was enjoying myself hugely when I noticed that the wind was carrying these dust clouds right through the open doors and into the school. I also noticed, to my discomfiture, that one of the teachers had seen the reason for the dust storm, and in high dudgeon ordered me to report to the principal. There, after explaining my presence, I felt the sharp sting of the rubber hose across my bottom. Thwack! a cloud of dust arose from my trousers. Wham! more dust. It was like beating a dirty carpet hanging on a clothesline. Every time he brought the hose down a puff of dust would rise up out of my trousers. I started to cry, and the tears traced a grimy path down my dust-laden cheeks. Mr. Kircher finally told me to go to the washroom, wash my face, and return to my class. It was a humiliating experience, especially to a boy who ordinarily got nothing but A's in deportment.

I can remember the name of my fifth-grade teacher, Miss Damon, simply because she had once told us that she expected us to forget her name as soon as we got out of the fifth-grade. Thinking back, maybe I wasn't such a paragon of virtue as I try to make myself believe, because I do remember Miss Damon forcing me to sit in front of the class with a stick of gum stuck to the end of my nose—her favorite punishment for those who chewed gum in class. She was a Carrie Nation type, and was forever preaching to us about the evils of drink and tobacco. She was, however, basically warm-hearted, loved the children, and was really a good teacher.

My dramatic career had its impetus in the sixth-grade when my teacher, Miss Wreebrecht, had me play the role of Scrooge in Dickens's Christmas Carol. I don't know whether she recognized my talents as a character actor, or whether she decided to give this unsympathetic role to the only Jewish boy in the class, but I enjoyed my debut as an actor and hammed it up thoroughly.

It was in the sixth-grade that I took my first manual training, a subject which I disliked intensely, and one in which I was undoubtedly the poorest student in the class. Years later I took an aptitude test which proved that, of all the professions, the one I was least likely to succeed in was carpentry, and my sixth-grade course in manual training bore this out. It took me all semester to finish my project, a simple broom holder, of which I was intently proud once I did manage to finish it. I must say that it did work. I screwed it on one of the walls of our summer kitchen, and for years afterward it served its purpose as a broom holder very well. That was about the only project I ever actually completed in manual training.

When I was about eight years old we moved from 1614 La Crosse Street to a house on Fifteenth Street. About a year later, we moved again, to 1516 Pine Street, where I lived during the rest of my life in La Crosse.

MR. COOPER
1916
(AGE 10)

Although I must have had at least a half dozen Hebrew teachers during various phases of my youth, there is one who stands out in my memory head and shoulders above the others. A character right out of the Old Testament, Mr. Cooper, a venerable old gentleman, white-haired, white-bearded, was an imposing figure who stood well over six feet tall, and carried himself straight as a sturdy old oak, despite his advanced age.

I can still picture Mr. Cooper sitting at the head of his class in the synagogue, sipping a glass of hot tea, with a long yardstick in one hand with which he didn't hesitate to rap the knuckles of those who were not paying strict attention. Nevertheless, he loved the children, and we in turn, respected and had a deep affection for him. Out of the mere pittance which he was paid, he would buy fruit for the children, and, almost daily, would purchase a supply of sweet corn which he would prepare for eating in a pail of boiling water, atop the pot-bellied stove which was used to heat the synagogue.

He would buy candies and pictured elementary Hebrew books, which he would distribute as prizes among the more accomplished of his students. My sister, Florence, was a favorite of his, and he would refer to her as his "Goote Keppele" (Good little head).

Mr. Cooper often lodged at our home, and it was during one of these periods that he gave mother his recipe for a perfectly delicious relish or piccalilli, with an eggplant base, which forever after was referred to in our home as "The Rebbes' Geshechte" or the Rabbi's Story.

In direct contrast to Mr. Cooper, as a teacher and as a man, was a certain Mr. Gahlenter, a middle-aged man, whose only physical features I remember were a set of large tobacco-stained buck teeth. He was a man given to telling off-color stories to some of the older students, and I disliked him intensely. I remember once when I was about twelve, he was visiting at our home when my sister Mary and I were the only ones at home. He and Mary were alone in the kitchen, while I was in the yard directly behind the kitchen letting my imagination run riot, as the imagination of a twelve year old often can. "If he attacks my sister, I'll rush in and defend her with this golf club," ran my thoughts, when suddenly I heard a terrific commotion coming from the kitchen. I rushed in, golf club clenched in my hand, ready to defend my sister's virtue with my life, only to find Mr. Gahlenter choking on a bit of strawberry preserve which he had been eating while sipping a glass of tea which my sister had been good enough to offer him. He was getting purple in the face when I entered. Mary was standing there, terrified, not knowing quite what to do. I started pounding him on the back, and luckily, after the first few thwacks, the piece of strawberry became dislodged, and he was soon back to normal. And that's as close as I ever came to fighting for the honor of one of my five sisters.

"Barefoot Boy with Cheeks of Tan"
1916
(Age 10)

John Greenleaf Whittier's "barefoot boy with cheeks of tan," upon whom he bestowed his benedictions, had nothing on me as an outdoorzy youngster. Come winter or summer, if I were not in school or at home eating my meals, I lived my life in the great out-of-doors. In the summertime I did without shoes and stockings as much as possible. I loved the feel of lush, green grass between my toes. Though I had to pay the penalty when crossing a field containing sand burrs, or when I inadvertently stepped on a bumble bee while looking for a lost golf ball in a field of clover, the joys of going barefoot outweighed by far its disadvantages.

La Crosse was an ideal town for a growing boy. Although I lived in the city, I was just five minutes from being a country boy with the aid of my trusty bike. During the winter months I knew the joys of ice skating on the lagoon, an overflow of the Mississippi River at the foot of the city, which when frozen over, formed a perfect ice skating rink. On the eastern outskirts of town there were many portions of hilly bluffs, unhampered by trees or underbrush, which were ideal for sledding or skiing. We would bring home-made skis made of barrel staves, upon which were nailed leather thongs into which we fit our feet, a contraption which made wonderful skis for us youngsters. The long, winding road which led up Grand Dad Bluff was ideal for sleds and toboggans after the first snowfall, so we had no lack of winter sports.

The first melting of the snows in early March was our cue to go foraging for the earliest of spring flowers, the sleek, fat, grey pussy-willows which we found growing among the rocky ledges of the bluffs. About the same time, or perhaps a little later, could be found hidden among the crevices of these same pussy-willow spots, the lovely, shy, half-hidden, sweet smelling violets, one of the early harbingers of spring. Then came the crocus or mayflower, found usually in the fields bordering the coulees. Why they were called mayflowers is beyond me, for they blossomed as a rule during the closing weeks of March or the first few weeks of April.

One of my favorites was also an early spring bloomer, the delicately shaded, lovely, pink and white Dutchman's britches (sic) which grew in profusion in the lowlands.

I would usually awaken before daylight on Memorial Day, or "Decoration" Day, as we called it, to make my way deep into a certain cool, damp coulee which fairly teemed with a variety of ferns of every description. These I would pluck, add a little color with bluebells, daffodils, or whatever I could find, arrange them in suitable bouquets, then head for Oak Grove Cemetery. By the time I got there, the annual Memorial Day parade would have reached the cemetery where it disbanded for the Memorial Day exercises, and I would sell my ferns at a quarter a bunch to those who wanted them to place on the graves. It was a lucrative business, and I usually cleaned up about five dollars for my efforts by noon, at which time I would head for the golf links where there was usually a Memorial Day tournament in progress. Between the sale of ferns and my caddying activities, Memorial Day was always a red-letter day for me financially.

During the summer months wildflowers grew in profusion in the coulees, and I knew just the best spots for them to be found. I had no compunction about picking them, because there were so many, and I had no feeling that I was depleting the supply. There was an abundance of honeysuckles, shooting stars, India pinks, and, deep in a cool, tree-bowered coulee through which the sun never penetrated, I knew just the spot for jack-in-the-pulpits. I once ran across a beautiful, black-spotted tiger lily, a plant which I did not pick, as I recognized its rarity, and figured that if I let the flower go to seed, there would be more next year. Somebody else must have figured differently, for when I searched for this plant the following year, it was gone.

I wrote earlier of how mother would never welcome these gifts of colorful flowers which I brought her. It wasn't that she didn't have an appreciation of the beauties of nature. At home she would plant nasturtiums, phlox, zinnias, and other flowers, and give them the tenderest of care, but my trips to the back country had other side products besides the flowers I brought—grass stains which must be washed out of my clothes, torn clothing which must be mended, the possibility of snake bites (there were plenty of snakes around). Anyhow, she preferred to discourage me from these jaunts into the wilds, and frankly, I don't blame her, although it did hurt my feelings at the time.

The autumn months brought with them trips of a more practical nature. I knew a spot where could be found delicious wild elderberries which I picked by the sackful, and from which my dad made delicious elderberry wine. There were berry patches of various types which grew wild, and I would get my share of them—blackberries, gooseberries, blueberries. We had to be especially careful of snakes on these berry-picking expeditions, as the bushes could easily hide a lurking reptile, and one of the boys had been bitten.

I learned that all nuts do nor grow on trees, that hazelnuts grow on bushes. A friend of mine, Lloyd Bieber, and I would make annual nutting treks, and gather our fill of hazelnuts and a varied assortment of walnuts which I would spread on our wood shed roof for drying in the sun. They made delicious winter eating.

Had I been a disciple of Audubon with ornithological leanings, La Crosse would have been an even greater treasure chest for me than it was. I was attracted only to those species which were the more flashily colored. I didn't have to leave my front yard to find English sparrows and robins. The raucous blue-jay and delicately tinted bluebird could also be found among the branches of the trees on our front lawn, while the riveting rata-tat-tat sound announced that a red-headed woodpecker was searching for food in a nearby tree trunk. I remember brightly plumaged scarlet tanagers and crimson cardinals in Myrick Park.

Also, many an early morning at the golf links I was greeted by the plaintive notes of the whippoorwill and the quick, piercing tones of "Bob white! Bob White!"

Yes, all year around there was outdoor excitement for a growing boy in the midwest town of La Crosse, Wisconsin. It was a happy, healthy, growing-up period, one which I wouldn't have exchanged for any other way of life for a growing boy.

VOLKOFF HOSPITALITY

Dad should have been a rich man. He would have made a wonderful philanthropist. He was forever bringing home for Sabbath dinners out-of-town visitors whom he met at the synagogue. Even in the early days at 1614 La Crosse Street, our home was considered an easy mark for a handout by the numerous hoboes who rode the rails and disembarked at a point where the train slowed down just a few blocks from our home. Our sidewalk and fence were always marked with mysterious chalk-marks which we later learned meant, "No dog—kind woman—good food."

We had a lot of guests especially during the religious holidays, and dad wasn't particular or choosy as to whom he invited. If they looked seedy or hungry or in need, their chances were so much the better. One night, for the Passover services, he brought home a man who, in these days, would have been a likely prospect for Alcoholics Anonymous. Part of the rites of the Passover services consists of taking frequent sips of wine after certain prayers are read—sips of wine, that is. This fellow evidently misinterpreted, and while we each took a dainty sip from our glass, he played "bottoms up" with his. We were too polite to protest, and dad would refill his glass each time, only to have it drunk to the last drop each time we took our sips. Finally, after he started to become tipsy, dad told him there was no more wine, but the damage had been done.

Dad really hit the jackpot when he met Marcus Rabinoff, a mercantile merchant from Wilton, Wisconsin, a little village about sixty miles from La Crosse. Mr. Rabinoff was a fine gentleman, a successful businessman, and he and dad soon became fast friends. As his was the only Jewish family in Wilton, he wished to spend the high holidays, Rosh Hashanah and Yom Kippur, in La Crosse, and was looking for lodging for his family. Dad insisted that they spend these holidays at our home, which would have been fine, except that his family consisted of seven daughters and one son in addition to his wife and himself. Well, they came…and kept coming year after year. Mother never protested, although the major portion of the baking and cooking for eighteen people, ten Rabinoffs and eight Volkoffs, was her responsibility.

How she did it, I don't know. Many times those holidays fell on the hottest week of the year, and to see her flushed face as she labored over that hot wood burner in the kitchen cooking a steaming mess of "gefilte" fish, working up a kettle full of chicken noodle soup, or baking a few extra loaves of bread, was not a pretty sight, when one considers that in these days, when the temperature gets up over eighty degrees, the modern housewife refuses to turn on the gas stove.

Sleeping was another problem. Our home contained four bedrooms; hardly enough for eighteen people. Most of us children slept on blankets on the floor in the living room or wherever space afforded, while the adults were given the luxury of the beds. Everything was in a state of bustle and turmoil, but nobody seemed to mind. Mother took it all in stride, and dad fairly beamed with the satisfied feeling that he was doing a good deed for a friend. I suppose there was some monetary agreement between the Rabinoffs and the Volkoffs—after all, there was an enormous amount of food consumed, but whatever the deal, I'm sure dad did no better than break even on it, and I frankly doubt if he did that.

For a time I considered Elizabeth Rabinoff, who was about my age, as my best girl friend. In fact, she was my first girl. I taught her how to roller-skate, let her ride my bike, and when she won the district championship in a declamatory contest, the finals of which were held at La Crosse Normal School, I was as proud as punch.

Throughout the year our home was seldom without a guest. A Mr. Brill, a novelty salesman who worked the fairs, was an annual guest at our home during County Fair week; itinerant rabbis would spend sometimes weeks at a time for practically no money as our guests. Dad was never so happy as when we were entertaining some stranger. Indeed, like Abou Ben Adem (may his tribe increase), dad's name is surely high on the list of those who love their fellow man.

World War I
1917-18
(Age 11-12)

The horrors of World War I seemed a long way off from us youngsters of the seventh and eighth grades back in those hectic years of 1917-'18. We were, however, well aware that there was a war in progress. Men in uniform were everywhere in evidence, and we all had relatives or close friends who were in the service. We saved our nickels, dimes, and quarters to buy Thrift Stamps which were later converted into Liberty Bonds. We went through meatless days and wheatless days without a whimper, and I even remember a tasteless concoction known as "potato ice cream." Each of us was given a plot of ground in an empty field near the school for our own personal "victory" garden, in which we raised an assortment of vegetables and did our best to keep the weeds from taking over.

It wasn't a bad war for us. Each Saturday afternoon we would go to the movies and see such thrillers as *To Hell With the Kaiser* or *The Beast of Berlin*. We hissed at Eric Von Stroheim in his roles of sadistic Prussian army officers, and we laughed at Charlie Chaplin in *Shoulder Arms*.

My bosom pal "Boodoo" Rosenfelt and I visited Camp Roberts, a military encampment just out of Sparta, Wisconsin, where "Boodoo" had an uncle who was an army officer. We slept overnight on a real army cot, had our meals at the officers' mess, and had a perfectly thrilling day. One of the officers offered us cigarettes, and when "Boodoo" accepted, there was nothing for me to do but follow suit. My experience with cigarettes at this point had been a few puffs of dried corn tassel wrapped in newspaper, so when they told me to, "Go ahead, inhale," I drew a deep breath and promptly started to choke. I thought I was dying, as I couldn't seem to get any air into my lungs. It was several moments before I was back to normal. It was a good experience for me, as I didn't go near a cigarette for ten years after that.

The bundles and sacks of magazines which dad brought home daily, together with his assorted metals and rags, proved fertile source of material for a war scrapbook which I compiled—a scrapbook of which I am still in possession—a scrapbook of war pictures in color. The covers of most magazines of the day were based on war themes, and periodicals such as *The Ladies Home Journal, The Red Cross Magazine, Saturday Evening Post*, and others, ran colorful sections of war pictures, all of which I cut out and added to my collection.

Several days before the armistice was signed there was a false report that the war was over. I remember mother rushing out to the playground one noon, shouting that the war was over. Where she received her news, I don't know, as there was no radio at the time. The newspaper must have put out an extra which a friend of hers must have read, and then phoned her. Anyhow, it was a false alarm, and the news of the real signing of the armistice did not reach us in La Crosse until late during the night of November 11th.

It must have been very late. I'm not sure, but I believe it was after midnight. I had long since gone to bed when I was awakened by whistles, bells ringing, the firing of guns, and the shouting of many people. Hurriedly I dressed and headed for the downtown section where most of the noise seemed to be originating. When I reached town, things were in a state of bedlam. The streets were crowded with flag-waving, singing, yelling townspeople gone delirious with joy. The war was over—the boys were coming home. It was a time to celebrate! It was a scene which I shall never forget, and one of which I was reminded twenty-seven years later in Hollywood, the day the Japanese surrendered in 1945. And so we rejoiced at the ending of "the war to make the world safe for Democracy," little dreaming that twenty-three years later we would be involved in another and more terrible holocaust.

La Crosse County Fair
or
Fly de Boids!
1919
(Age 13)

The red-letter week of the year for those of us who lived within walking distance of the fairgrounds was the annual La Crosse County Fair week. The excitement started for us several days before the fair actually got under way with the arrival of the various forms of livestock which were to be exhibited. Heralded by the huffing and puffing of smoke belching steam engines pulling the cattle-cars along a seldom used railroad siding adjacent to the fairgrounds, we neighborhood youngsters, attracted like flies to a sugar bowl by the arrival of the livestock, would swarm to the siding, yelling excitedly, "Cattle! Cattle! The Cattle-cars are coming."

We would watch the unloading with bated breath, especially if some high strung prize bull with a brass ring through its nose was being led through the chutes. It was fun also to watch the unloading of the swine, for there was always one or two of the pigs which would get loose and, squealing and grunting, would lead their pursuers in a merry chase before they were recaptured. If the proceedings went along too tamely, there were always two or three of the more adventurous among us who would not hesitate to use well-aimed sling shots to stir up the animals a bit, to the consternation of their keepers. Dairy cows and bulls, all manner of swine, sheep, goats, chickens, and doves were transported to the fair from all over the state by train, as this was before the days of good roads when a good portion of these exhibits could be brought in by truck.

Although the utilitarian purpose of the fair was to exhibit produce and livestock, and win honor, distinction, and blue ribbons for the farmer, the real glitter and glamour of the fair was the Midway, with its carnival acts, fun-rides, and various concessions. One attraction which was present for a good many years was Singer's Midgets, grown men and women shorted than we children who gawked at them in fascination.

Then there was the ever present "girlie" act, a feature without which no carnival Midway was complete. The girls would do their "teaser" on a platform in front of their tent, singing and dancing to one of the current hits of the day, such as, *Will you be my little baby bumblebee, buzz around, buzz around, buzz around.*" There would be the obviously faked thrill acts—"See Bobo, half man, half lion, direct from the wilds of Borneo. From inside the tent could be heard the terrifying roar of a lion. When one paid his dime or quarter to see this lurid creature, he was confronted by a—perfectly ordinary man wearing a mangy lion skin, and rubbing on a taut tendon of some sort to produce the roars.

I remember one season when Ripley's "Believe It Or Not" troupe played the fair, and here were some really legitimate thrillers. There was also the Sports Arena where overweight wrestlers huffed and puffed and tugged and pulled at each other in displays of athletic prowess which were much less thrilling than their modern counterparts in the person of Gorgeous George, Wild Red Berry, and the like.

All of these various attractions were highlighted by the magic spiel of the Midway barker, "Hurry, hurry, hurry. It's never out, it's never over—One thin dime takes you all the way through—There's a cow in there with two heads—See that wild man from Borneo, half man, half beast—Hurry, hurry, hurry!!" Then, of course, the spiel of the concessionaires, "Win your girl a kewpie doll…round and round she goes, and where she stops, nobody knows." Or "Get your red, red, red-hots." A cacophony of exciting sounds which held an intriguing fascination for me.

One afternoon, after having gorged myself with hot dogs, peanuts, popcorn, and salt-water taffy, all washed down with strawberry pop, I unwisely decided to take a ride on "The Whip", a fun-ride which whipped one around in jerky moves capable of unsettling even an empty stomach. Mine, far from empty. revolted. and I became violently ill. To this day, I am unable to look a fun-ride in the face without becoming nauseous. My limit now is the merry-go-round or the Ferris wheel.

I always liked to feel that I was part of the show during County Fair week, so I usually got myself some sort of job at the fair. One season I sold cold drinks in the grandstand. "Ice-cold pop, hear! Get your ice-cold soda pop!" This enabled me to watch the free acts in front of the grandstand, which were usually of the thriller, trapeze, high-wire variety. I also got a thrill out of the trotting and pacing horse races which were a daily feature at each fair.

The first year in which prohibition went into effect I sold a non-alcoholic beer-like drink called Bevo, which did a big business at a quarter a bottle. This was in connection with a soft drink concession which was operated by the Levy brothers, Meyer, Sam, and Louie, a most aggressive trio of youngsters who were real go-getters and considered by those who knew them as potential big businessmen. While still in their teens they were in charge of the out-of-town Sunday Newspaper distribution in La Crosse, and had the soft drink concessions tied up at the fair, athletic contests, and other affairs.

On year, "Boodoo" Rosenfelt and I got a job with a man who ran a novelty stand selling souvenirs of the fair, pennants, post cards, buttons, kewpie dolls, and a contraption which consisted of a stick to which was tied an imitation canary which flapped its wings and whistles as the stick was waved around. This particular gentleman believed in keeping his help occupied so, during slack periods, he would yell at us to "Fly de boids! Fly de boids!" We would swish those imitation birds vigorously through the air in an effort to drum up more trade.

JOE, THE CADDY
(1915-1921)

From the time I was nine years old, when "Boodoo" Rosenfeld arranged an interview for me with Art Bakkum, caddymaster at the La Crosse Country Club, which resulted in the beginning of my career as a caddy, the compelling, outstanding interest, the one great love of my boyhood days, was the golf links. During the spring and autumn months I couldn't wait for the end of the school day so I might hop on my bike and make my way to the links. During the summer months I was there from dawn to dusk, and I spent many a winter day trudging over the snow-covered fairways, wishing wistfully for the return of springtime.

Members of the country club were proud of their beautiful nine hole, par 37 course, which lay nestled at the foot of the bluffs and dipped into the coulees which lay just east of the city. It was a well kept, well constructed course, whose greens were like velvet, whose fairways were always well groomed, and whose carefully planned bunkers, sand traps, and ditches, made it a sporty, rather difficult links to play.

The La Crosse Country Club was not an exclusive rich man's club. Most of the leading citizens of La Crosse were members—professional men, business men, as well as members of the teaching staff of the La Crosse State Teachers' College. It provided an ideal method for a growing lad to earn his spending money, for besides offering healthful exercise in the open air, it gave us youngsters an opportunity to rub elbows with the cream of La Crosse citizenry and make personal contacts which, later in life, were of tremendous value. In my own case, I got my start with the La Crosse Theaters Company (which was really my start in show business) through Frank L. Koppelberger who owned the company and for whom I caddied for many years.

Early in the summer of my first year as a caddy, as I was nearing my ninth birthday, dad bought three bicycles for his children—two girl's bikes, without the crossbar, for the use of his five daughters, and one beautiful, shiny, red and white Dixie Flyer which was exclusively for me. It was a fine vehicle, sturdily constructed, with the latest type brakes, with a real leather seat, and a loud, jangly bell. Dad had paid forty dollars for this two-wheeled marvel, and told me he expected me to repay him out of my earnings as a caddy. I'm proud to say that bike was paid for before the winter snows set in. For years this bike was my inseparable companion. As the links were several miles from our home, it was a great help in getting me out there. The only reason I didn't ride it to grade school was that the school was located just across the alley from our home. Later I did use it to get me to high school. Of course, we didn't have the traffic conditions to contend with in 1915 that we have today, but when I think back to some of the stunts I used to pull it makes my hair stand on end. For instance, on the way to the golf links I would sometimes hitch a ride with some club member who was driving out. By "hitch a ride", I mean that I held on to the car with one hand while I steered the bicycle with the other. The roads those days were mostly tarred, and not as smooth as today's, and I bumped along with no thought for the danger which attended those bumps. If my son would even think of using a bicycle in this manner, it would scare me half to death, but I never gave it a thought.

When I first became a caddy, the fees were twenty-five cents for nine holes, fifty cents if we carried "double"; that is, caddied for two players at the same time. Soon after my debut, the boys, under the leadership of "Boodoo", decided to strike for more money. Their demands were to double the fees, fifty cents for nine holes and one dollar for nine holes "double". I was against the idea from the start. As a nine year old, I felt the pay I received was satisfactory, and I was loathe to take the chance of being fired for having the temerity to strike, especially so soon after I first became a caddy. But, as the other boys were all for it, I reluctantly agreed to go along. It was exciting. The strike began Saturday morning. We marched in a body along a dirt road paralleling the golf links, jeering at the players carrying their own bags. Most of the club members waved good-naturedly back at us, highly amused by this juvenile demonstration. That afternoon Art Bakkum called in "Boodoo", "Wissy" Marquart, "Mart" Robare, and others of the ringleaders for a conference, offering a compromise pay raise of five cents which would bring the fees up to thirty cents for nine holes, sixty cents for eighteen, double the pay for carrying double. Without argument the boys accepted and went back to work. The strike was over, but I was furious. I didn't want to strike in the first place, but I figured as long as we made the plunge, we shouldn't have capitulated at the first offer made to us. We should at least have held out for forty cents. I refused to sign the pact, and for two days stayed away from the golf links, the only holdout of the entire group. When I finally sheepishly gave in, Art was very nice to me and, in fact, congratulated me for sticking to what I thought was right. This reaction showed an obstinate streak in me which my wife claims I never did get rid of.

I took several years to develop into a good caddy. Those of us who took our jobs seriously, studied each member's likes and dislikes, and got to know just what club he preferred for any given situation. For instance, we knew that "Tubby" Keeler, the powerfully built athletic coach of the Teachers' College used a mashie niblick to drive from the 178 yard third hole, while others, less hefty of build, would use a mid-iron, brassie, or even a driver. We learned which members preferred their caddies to be seen and not heard, and which ones liked a bit of advice occasionally such as, "You didn't keep your head down, sir." or, "Your left elbow should be kept closer to your body on the backswing, sir. That's what caused you to slice on your last shot." Some members liked to have their caddies help them keep score, and some, especially the women, instructed their caddies to keep tab on their opponent's score. We learned just the proper time to pull the flag from the hole on the green, how to stand so that our shadow didn't fall across the ball as a player was making his shot, and most important, how to mark the spot where a ball had disappeared into the rough so that we could easily locate it. The unforgivable sin was to lose a ball for the player for whom we were caddying, and we took a great deal of pride in our ability in this respect. I would even occasionally call upon Deity to assist me in the all-important task of locating a lost ball, murmuring fervently, "Please God, help me find this ball, and I promise I'll be a good boy all summer long." More often than not, God would come through.

On Monday mornings the caddies were allowed to play golf themselves until nine o'clock. I would get there each Monday just at the break of dawn so as to take advantage of every available moment, so that by nine o'clock I had been able to play at least eighteen holes, sometimes more. That early in the morning the grass was usually heavily covered with dew, and we would play barefooted so as not to get our shoes or stockings wet. Even rain would not deter us, and many a Monday morning saw the links dotted with golf-playing caddies, sloshing through a steady downpour or a veritable cloudburst or thunder storm, so anxious were we not to miss our Monday morning golfing privileges.

A caddies tournament was held annually in which the winning caddies were presented with prizes of golf clubs and balls. I was not a particularly good player, but as tournaments were handicap affairs, we all felt that we had a chance. I remember one year, in my first match, I was pitted against the caddy champion, Willis "Wissy" Marquart, who was really an excellent golfer. However, I was to get a stroke a hole from him, which is quite a handicap, and I felt I had some chance. It was an eighteen hole match, and at the end of the first nine I was three up on "Wissy", having traversed the course in forty-six strokes (which was playing way over my head, as I rarely broke fifty in my regular Monday morning play). We tied the first hole of the second nine, but when Austin Fingerhoot, one of the caddies in our foursome, leaned over to me and whispered, "You don't really believe you can beat "Wissy", do you?", it must have had a psychological effect, for, from that point on, I really couldn't believe that I could defeat the champ, even with that terrific handicap. He beat me, two up and one to go, although he played a one under par thirty-six in order to do so, setting a new caddy record. Ironically, he did not win the tournament that year, as he was defeated in the finals by "Boy" Nuffke who, though not as spectacular a player as "Wissy", was the steadier of the two. "Boy" had an added advantage in that he caddied steady for an old gentleman who played alone each afternoon and allowed his caddy to play along with him.

My favorite "steady" was Frank L. Koppelberger, owner and manager of the La Crosse Theaters Company, and his wife Dora. Not only were they nice people to work for, but "Kop" was a good tipper, and would often hand me a dollar bill instead of the usual sixty cents after nine holes of carrying for him and his wife. During certain periods when there was a shortage of caddies, I would hide in a ravine at the edge of the first hole until the Koppelbergers showed up, then run out and take their bags. Otherwise, as it was first come first served, I would have been compelled to caddy for some members who had arrived before them. On the few occasions when some other caddy carried their bags (when I was late or still out on the links with an earlier job), I was heartbroken. Years later, while working for the La Crosse Theaters Company, I overheard a couple of vaudevillians berating Mr. Koppelberger for using sharp business tactics in his dealing with them. They disliked him heartily, and I was shocked to find that my idol, a man who in my mind could do no wrong, had feet of clay. Mr. Koppelberger, who took up golf for his health, grew to love the game dearly and would usually play eighteen holes each afternoon with some crony, and then, after dinner, another nine with his wife and some other couple. Those last nine holes, just before nightfall, in the cool of the evening, after a hot summer day, were really enjoyable, even for a tired caddy.

Tournament days, especially the tournaments in which our club members would compete against visiting members from other cities, were the highlights of the season. We would have tournaments with Winona, Sparta, and other adjacent towns; but the really big tournament of the year was with Madison when our club would play host to visiting golfers from Wisconsin's capitol city. I caddied for a couple of university professors during one of these tournament days, at the end of which they tipped me liberally and told me I was full of "keen acumen and perspicacity!" We liked to caddy for these visitors, but were fiercely loyal to our own club members, and were always very much interested in the big match of the day between our pro and the visiting pro. "Chick" Frazier, who was the pro when I first broke in as a caddy, was about the best playing pro we had.

When our club members were hosted by other clubs in their own tournaments, we would do our best to make the trip, either by bike or accepting a car ride from some generous local golfer. About five of us, the Ristow brothers, Hans Stein, Sam Katz, and I had formed a bicycle club, and proudly adopted as our motto, "We Pass Fords!" We would cycle to Winona, Minnesota, a town about thirty miles from La Crosse, and I must say we weren't welcomed too heartily by the Winona caddies. However, there were usually enough of us, and we stuck together, so that they never started any serious trouble.

I am ashamed to say that several of the caddies occasionally took advantage of visiting golfers who trustingly left new golf balls in the pockets of their caddy bags. The temptation to filch one or two was too great and many a player left town with fewer balls in his possession than he had brought with him. Although I was never tempted to steal golf balls, there was one occasion when I did act in a manner somewhat less than honorable, although I felt I was justified in what I did. I was caddying for a couple of young, empty-headed socialites who kept up a constant stream of inane prattle as they played. When we were on the fourth hole, one of them said, "If there's anything I can't stand, it's Jews and niggers!" Her partner agreed with her. I was simply furious. My first inclination was to drop their bags, walk off, and let them caddy for themselves. I thought better of this, for I would have undoubtedly been fired for insubordination—I would have been biting off my nose to spite my face. But I decided I must do something to avenge myself on them for their snobbery and bigotry and I quickly decided on how I could get even with them. Every time they drove a ball into a ditch, I stepped it into the muck and pretended I couldn't find it. When a ball went into the rough, I conveniently had trouble locating it. I lagged behind, made then wait for their clubs, violated every precept of good caddying, and made them wonder why on earth they ever chose me as their caddy that day. I can assure you, they never asked for me again. It may have been dishonest, but I felt I had every right to act as I did.

Among the colorful characters who played golf at the La Crosse Country Club in those days was young Carly Van Auken, barely out of his teens, a chubby bundle of energy who did most of his playing alone, simply because he could rarely find a partner who could keep up with him. Carly fairly raced around the links, taking giant, almost running strides. It took the average player well over an hour to complete the nine holes, but Carly made it in just over thirty minutes. This, coupled with the fact that he had an unusually large bag well-filled with clubs, a caddy-killer, made him quite unpopular with the caddies, and we would attempt to duck out of sight when Art brought his bag out, for we knew that whoever carried his bag was due for an exhaustive nine holes. Eighteen holes with Carly would mean a pooped out caddy, no good for any more work the rest of that day. Carly had an older brother, George, who was a much more conservative character and a better player, a man who was club champion for many years.

Homer Hart was a man who had an uncontrolled slice which he couldn't get rid of, so, finally, in desperation, he just regulated his stance to allow for it, with good results. It was funny to watch him addressing his ball as though he were aiming at a spot way to the left of the green, have the ball start off way too far to the left but invariably start curving until it finished right on the green.

Another grand old gentleman was a dentist, Dr. Gatterdam, who loved the game, and who wasn't a bad golfer. He was nervous in front of an audience, though, and I remember one Madison Tournament day when there was quite a group of players waiting to tee off on the first hole. Doc took a nervous swipe at the teed-up ball and missed it completely. His second shot hit a railroad track about fifty yards away and bounced back almost to the tee. Poor Doc—he had a devil of a time getting started in that match, but to his credit, I must say he overcame his initial nervousness and finally won his match.

Golf is a game which tends to bring out a man's real character. I have seen staid old bank presidents cheat on their score. I have seen a man holding a good job deliberately throw a match to his opponent, who just happened to be his boss.

During the war years, 1917 and '18, we would get a real thrill caddying for servicemen from nearby camps who would visit the club for a round or two of golf when on furlough. Many of the members enlisted or were drafted into the service. My particular hero was Ken Saltzer of the Saltzer Seed Company, who was in the air force, one of the few flyers from La Crosse. When I visited the links briefly while in the mid-west in 1954, almost forty years later, I saw Ken, and outside of a few grey hairs and a little added weight, he hadn't changed much in appearance. On that same visit, I also was surprised to see that "Wissy" Marquart had justified his position as the number one caddy by growing up to become the club pro. We had a delightful time reminiscing about the old days.

There was an abundance of many types of snakes which inhabited the bluffs and coulees adjacent to the golf course, and often they would slither their way to the fairways. One morning we found a large rattlesnake with about ten rattles attached to his tail. It had just made a meal of a gopher which it had swallowed whole, head first, and we could just see the gopher's tail protruding from the snake's distended jaws. The snake was helpless and was easily disposed of with a mashie niblick. Grass snakes were a common variety found there, and some of the kids would put them in their pockets and get a great kick out of taking them to school to scare the teacher and the girls.

While Carly Van Auken held the record as the fastest player at the course, the group who comprised the Sunday Morning syndicate gang was by far the slowest. Made up of non-church-going members of the club who had a penchant for gambling, this group of eight to twelve players would play what they called "cutthroat" syndicates. That is, the player with the lowest score would collect chips from all the others, the second lowest scorer on each hole would collect from all those with higher scores, and so on, which meant that the poor fellow with the highest score had to pay all the others. As they usually played for a dollar a chip, this sometimes ran into big money. Usually they scored according to their individual handicaps, giving each other strokes, which meant that at the end of each hole, more time was consumed in figuring out who owed who what than it took to actually play the hole. It took the group about three hours to traverse nine holes. They would then break for lunch, and play another nine in the afternoon. It was interesting and exciting, caddying for this group. If I was lucky, and was carrying double for two of the top winners of the group, I was assured of a hefty tip. However, if I had the losers, I worked those long hours just for scale.

I'll never forget the day Walter Hagen and Joe Kirkwood, Jr., the great trick shot artist, came to town. They played as a foursome—Hagen, Kirkwood, and the two best club golfers, George Van Auken and Russ Thompson. There was a large gallery who had paid to watch these two world renowned golfing figures, and four of the best caddies were selected to carry the bags. "Wissy", who was recognized as the number one caddy, carried for Walter Hagen, "Boy" Nuffke was Kirkwood's boy, Herb Ristow carried for Russ Thompson, and I completed the foursome as George Van Auken's caddy. We were the proudest boys in America that Saturday afternoon to have been so honored and were really on our toes during that eighteen hole exhibition. Hagen, one of the greatest showmen in all golfdom, put on a brilliant exhibition, and Kirkwood followed the regular exhibition with a display of trick shots that were truly amazing. With his almost perfect control over that elusive little pellet, it is hard to understand why he didn't make better showings in the big national tournaments in which he participated. He explained it by stating that he was probably lacking in a certain quality known as "competitive spirit".

Minneapolis Interlude
1923 (Age 17)

Dad had long wanted to get out of the junk business. With five daughters either at or approaching the marriageable age, he felt that a junk-man father would impede considerably their chances of a favorable marriage. Also, a city the size of La Crosse offered little opportunity for a Jewish maiden to choose a mate. So, early that summer, soon after I had graduated from high school, dad disposed of his horse and wagon, his accumulation of metals, papers, and rags, sold our home at 1516 Pine Street, and set out with his family to make a new start in Minneapolis, where my two sisters, Sally and Marion, had already matriculated a year or two previous.

The year we spent in Minneapolis was not a particularly happy one, either for dad, for mother, for the girls, and especially, for me. Dad had no business experience, besides that of the junk business, and it took him months to decide on what type of business he would invest his life savings. It was finally decided that he buy a grocery store in a rather shabby part of town, one which, the owner presumable had been doing a good business, but which he had decided to sell because of poor health.

The grocery store proved to be a headache almost from the start. Dad knew nothing of the tricks of the trade, had no feeling for which items were salable, couldn't say "no" to a salesman, and often stocked up on items which lay on the shelves for months. If dad wasn't a good businessman, I turned out to be a chip off the old block. I hated the store. My years of outdoor life caddying at the golf links, and the taste of show business I had from working for the La Crosse Theaters Company, had spoiled me for working behind a counter with merchandise which meant a penny profit on this item, and possible three cents on that. Like dad, who was too honest and trusting for his own good, I would allow perfect strangers to open charge accounts, without checking on their credit standing or ability to pay. I remember once, a dapper, nice-looking young fellow came into the store and wished to open an account. I not only let him open the account on the strength of his friendly attitude, but instead of keeping his initial purchases down to bare necessities until we had checked on him, I tried to sell him everything in sight. I should have become suspicious when he bought everything I suggested, even a big basket of luscious concord grapes. I was proud of my success as a salesman until, after several weeks had passed in which we hadn't heard from him. I went to the address he had given me and found that nobody by the name had ever resided there.

After several months behind the counter, it was decided that I was not cut out to be a successful grocery clerk. My sister, Sally, quit her job at a bank to devote her full time helping mother and dad at the store. I, meanwhile, had gotten myself a job as an order filler at the Sharood Mail Order Company. It was like jumping from the frying pan into the fire. At the store, I could at least take it easy. Business was never too brisk, and the hours passed at a leisurely rate. At Sharood's there was no such thing as leisure. Order fillers were given a sheaf of orders to be filled in a certain length of time. My first day, determined to make good, I really concentrated on my work, and couldn't quite understand it when one of the girl wrappers whispered to me, "Don't be such an eager beaver." However, I soon found out what she meant. If I was originally given, say, thirty orders to fill in an hour, my quota for the next hour was raised to thirty-five. If I could handle this amount, the quota was again stepped up until I was always about five short of filling each batch at the end of the hour, even though I worked at top speed. As you can well imagine, at a mail order house we filled orders for everything from thumb tacks to overcoats. In order to increase our speed, we worked on roller skates—sometimes a pair, but mostly only one, with the skateless foot to push. I would come home exhausted, but the recuperative powers of a seventeen year-old are truly startling, and after a hot dinner, I was off for an evening at one of the numerous ice-skating rinks which flourished in Minneapolis.

The Sharood Mail Order Company was a long street-car ride (including a couple of transfers) from where I lived, and I remember one icy winter's day, I reached home with the tip of my nose frozen; small wonder, for it was forty degrees below zero in Minneapolis that day. It really gets cold in Minneapolis during the winter months.

It was during this period that I became acquainted with a group of A.Z.A. boys who were really junior members of the B'nai Brith. They had organized a basketball team and invited me to join them. Although I wasn't fast enough to be a good player, I had developed a pretty fair shooting eye from years of practice shooting on the Washington School playgrounds. The first practice session I attended, I was given a chance to display my ability towards the end of the period. I wasn't particularly setting the world on fire, but just before the close of the session, I found myself with the ball at about half-court. From a team standpoint, I should have passed the ball to one of my teammates and thus work the ball closer to the basket. I decided to try for a long one. I arched the ball high into the air, and it swished down through the hoop without even touching the rim. "Boy, what an eye! We can use this fellow," and other laudatory remarks greeted me, and I felt that I was in, I was accepted, I was part of the team. But fate would have it otherwise. The very next morning I awoke with swollen toes, the doctor was summoned, ignored my toes, but looked down my throat and gave his verdict—my tonsils had to come out. This was the beginning of a rheumatic-arthritic condition for which, during the past thirty-five years, I have tried every known remedy. I have had my tonsils removed twice (the first time they were evidently just clipped, and grew right back again); I have had mud baths in Waukesha, Wisconsin, and hot spring baths at Hot Springs, Arkansas; I have had gold in oil emulsion, bee sting treatments, and have been hospitalized for a sinus condition when there was nothing wrong with my sinus according to a clinic of Memphis, Tennessee physicians. I have been pummeled by chiropractors, twisted and stretched by osteopaths. I have been placed on special diets (including a three day water diet followed by a week of nothing but ground liver.) I do not have a single tooth in my head which I can call my own. One by one they have come out in the hope that this one might be the offender which has been poisoning my body all these years. I once paid forty dollars for a leather and steel harness-like contraption to be worn as a brace on my back, but it proved so unwieldy and uncomfortable that after a week I hung it up in the closet, and it has long since disappeared.

When the wonder drugs made their appearance and cortisone was effecting some marvelous cures among arthritics, I thought this might be the answer, but, alas, I soon learned that cortisone was effective only for the relief of rheumatoid-arthritis, and my affliction was the type over which cortisone had no jurisdiction.

I am somewhat consoled by the fact that my condition has become stabilized, and, though my posture isn't what it should be, and I look rather stooped (not stupid!), I suffer no pain, my movements are fairly unhampered, and feel that if I must, I can live with it without undue discomfort.

But to get back to Minneapolis—the store had been losing money steadily, and it was thought best to get out form under as gracefully as possible. The original owner had evidently recovered his health for he agreed to buy back the store, and it was decided to write off the year's losses to experience, and for the family to return to La Crosse where dad was to return to the only business he knew anything about—the junk business. I and my two younger sisters, Rose and Bertha, were to return to school. Sally and Marion would remain in Minneapolis, and Florence was, I believe, to begin her teaching career. Dad was able to buy back the very house in which we had lived for so many years at 1516 Pine Street by paying the owners five thousand dollars more than they had paid him when he sold it to them, and life resumed an even keel.

There was one last episode which was in keeping with most everything else that happened during that ill-fated year. When dad finally made the deal to sell the store, he was so happy to get out from under that he gave the new owner a set of duplicate keys to the store before the deal had been consummated, even before an inventory had been taken of the stock on hand. Mother was horrified. How could he do such a foolish thing? Why, he was practically inviting the man to rob us. She had much the better business head of the two, and was probably right—if the man were dishonest, he could easily have opened the store after hours and spirited away some valuable merchandise. So she made life miserable for poor, trusting, old dad, until he went practically out of his mind, all because, from his viewpoint, he was trying to show goodwill towards the new owner. As it turned out, no harm was done, and the gentleman had no idea of trying to cheat us out of anything, but it was a terrible period for dad who had tried so hard to make things work out. I'm sure he was glad to get back to the comparative peace and quiet of small town life. Never one to keep up with progress, he should have bought a truck when he returned to start life anew at the same old stand, but no, it was again a wagon and horse. He loved regal names for his horses—this one he named Rex.

La Crosse State Homecoming
With Volkoff horse, Blackie
The Volkoff horse in a football parade. The sign reads—
BEN HUR-rying back to
HOMECOMING

JOE, THE READER

The La Crosse Public Library was a truly important cog in my mental development, even in my pre-reading days. Every Saturday morning, while I was in kindergarten and first grade, escorted by one of my sisters, I would hurry to the library to be one of thirty or forty children seated on the floor in a semi-circle in front of one of the librarians while she regaled us with tales of Cinderella, Little Red Riding Hood, and other childhood favorites. I would listen in wrapt (sic) attention, and could hardly wait until I could learn to read so that I could wrest these delightful tales for myself from the printed page.

From the time that I could figure out one word from another, from the days that I thrilled to Little Half Chick or Chicken-Licken, I was an omnivorous reader. I don't believe I missed a book from the children's department of the library. First, the simple little tales out of the vividly colored First Readers, then the Grimm's Fairy Tales, the sugar-coated geography series entitled Our Little Cousins from Other Lands, and as I grew older, the myriad books of adventure: Robin Hood, Robinson Crusoe, Tom Sawyer, and all the rest of them. I even went for the girl's books—Mrs. Wiggs of the Cabbage Patch, Mother Carey's Chickens, and Heidi, which was a particular favorite of mine. I was right with Toby Tyler when he ran away to join the circus, and lived every moment with the adventurous Swiss Family Robinson. It was at the library that I met most of our national heroes: Washington, Lincoln, the Greene Mountain Boys, Daniel Boone, Davey Crockett, Kit Carson. I lived those last moments with the heroic Texans at the Alamo and charged with Teddy Roosevelt up San Juan Hill. The Ralph Henry Barbour books of young athletic heroes were great favorites of mine, probably because I was not an athletic type and got a vicarious thrill playing the hero as I read. It was at the public library that I first became acquainted with "The Youth's Companion", "Boy's Life", and "The American Boy", and I would spend many a winter afternoon seated at one of the round tables in the children's room eagerly devouring the contents of these magazines. Yes, the public library played an integral part in my early education.

But I had another source to help satisfy my insatiable demand for reading material. Each day, when my dad would come home with his wagon full of bundles and sacks of magazines which he had collected during the day, I would search through this treasure trove to come up with types of literature not to be found in the public library. It was here, in the back of the wagon, that I first met Nick Carter, one of the greatest detectives of them all, and it was here I was first introduced to such doughty characters as Frank Merriwell, boy athlete of Yale, Fred Fearnot, with muscles of steel beneath that calm exterior, to the Westerns of that era, Young Wild West and Arietta, to Buffalo Bill and other paper-covered thrillers. And then, of course, there were the Horatio Alger books, <u>Sink or Swim</u>, <u>Tim</u>, <u>The Bootblack</u>, <u>Up from Poverty</u>, and all the rest of that series which so inspired the youth of that era. I never could understand why the library didn't carry those books, until I ran across one years later and could see then that they were not exactly literary classics. To this generation, they would probably seem corny and not at all interesting, but to us they were tops and sold in the millions. I never did read the Rover Boys, the Tom Swift series, and others of their ilk for two reasons—the library didn't carry them, and those who owned them must have thought a lot of them, for I never found them in my dad's wagon.

During my teens I got to be a short story addict since my dad brought home plenty of pulp magazines, including Argosy, All Story, Red Book, Blue Book, Western Story, and Sport Story. My favorite among the slicks was Cosmopolitan, which then featured stories by such famous writers as Pearl Buck, Edna Farber, Octavus Roy Cohen, and Irvin Cobb.

After the war came a flood of war books, most of which I read, but only one of which still stands out in my memory—Sergeant Guy Empys <u>Over the Top</u>. I even remember one line from the book, "Over the top, with the best of luck, and give 'em Hell!" It was exciting reading. It was all exciting in those days, and I'm thankful both for the facilities of the library and the opportunities to explore my dad's wagon, both of which contributed towards a fuller and richer life for me.

Joe, The Sports Enthusiast

Most of the athletic thrills of my life have been vicarious ones, as I have long been a spectator sports enthusiast. That doesn't mean that I didn't like to participate—I did. But I was never more than mediocre in my attempts, although I got a kick out of trying.

Take football, for instance. When I was ten or eleven years of age, I was rather slow and pudgy, and when the boys chose up sides for a game, I was the last one picked. However, when a group in our neighborhood organized a team which they called "The Goosetown Bearcats," inasmuch as several of the team members lived in a section of town on the wrong side of the tracks known as Goosetown, it was a question of including me in or having only ten "men" of the eleven. They put me in at guard, which was then considered the least important position on the team. I was so anxious to make good, to conform and be accepted as one of them by the rest of the boys, that I played way over my head, made some good tackles, opened up holes for our backfield, and succeeded so well that the next season, because I had the weight and the will, was promoted to fullback, a position I held during the next few years until the Bearcats disbanded.

Perhaps the best tackle I ever made in my life occurred during a practice in a playground near our home. We had just kicked off to the opposition when I noticed that dad was returning home from work, his wagon in an alleyway just a few feet from the playground. He was in a position to observe the play very well. I rushed at the ball carrier, hit him solidly with my shoulder, twined my arms about his lower body, then slid them down in the most approved fashion around his legs, and we plunged to earth among the sandburrs in a cloud of dust. While I was receiving the plaudits of my teammates, I glanced covertly over my shoulder to see what impression I had made on dad, ready to wave matter-of-factly to him, as though this was just my usual performance. Alas, he hadn't even noticed that I was there—he was looking the other way, deeply engrossed, perhaps, in the current price of metals. My sterling performance had been in vain. And yet, I think dad could have been a sports enthusiast, if he were not so wrapped up in attempting to make both ends meet in supporting a family of eight. He took me to the county fair one day when I was about eight, and the first place for which he headed was the sports arena where a couple of third rate wrestlers were tugging and pulling at each other. His voice was raised just as loud as the others in calling the attention of the referee to some foul tactic of the villain in the piece, and he yelled loudest of all when the underdog finally won the match. So I'm sure I could have made a football or baseball fan out of him, given half a chance.

I marvel now that we teenagers didn't receive more broken bones and suffer more serious injuries than we did. Most of our games were played in the late fall, with the ground hardened by the nip of frost. We wore no helmets, no shoulder or hip pads, no protective gear of any sort, and we played hard, rough ball. I often came home bruised and battered, but never anything serious.

I went out for high school football in my senior year, when I was sixteen, but Coach Keogan only laughed at me. "If you had come out when you were a sophomore, I would have been glad to work with you," he said, "but now why should I waste my time trying to develop you? Next year you'll be out of here. I'm looking for men who can help me next year and the year after!" Of course, if I had gone out for high school football when I was a sophomore, when I was fourteen, and not large for my age, it would have been murder, for some of those high school varsity men were both big and fast.

As for other forms of athletics, I did a lot of swimming as a child, but never learned to swim well. If there is any one worthwhile thing we did for our son, David, it was to see that he learned to swim properly at an early age. We sent him to the Curtis Swim School, where he learned how to execute the Australian crawl in a proper manner, developed a beautiful stroke, and did so well that he eventually earned his letter in high school as a member of the varsity swimming squad. I, on the other hand, learned the hit-or-miss method. We would go swimming either in the Mississippi River at the "bath house", a public swimming spot at the foot of the city, or, more often, in the La Crosse River, down the track, over the trestle, and around the bend, where there was a hidden cove where we could swim without benefit of bathing suit. The water was mostly below our shoulders, except for one spot about ten feet across which was over our heads. We could easily have laid flat and let the current carry us over this spot, but it gave me much more satisfaction and feeling of accomplishment to paddle furiously, dog-fashion, until we were beyond the bounds of the step-off. It was only the daring ones who were the really good swimmers who would attempt to cross that spot against the current. I never even made the attempt.

Golf? I was a self-made, unschooled golfer—or was I? I used to spend hours lying in the shade of the old elm trees on the practice fairway, listening with both ears wide open as the current "pro" gave golfing lessons to one of the members. It was here I picked up the fine points of the game, the proper stance, the overlapping grip, left arm close to the body on the back-swing, head down, eyes on the ball, and all the hundred and one things a good golfer gets to know instinctively. By the time I was seventeen, I was a fairly good golfer, loved the game, played in the low eighties and very occasionally broke eighty. I played a lot of golf while I was in Memphis, but since I came to California in 1937, although I brought a set of clubs with me, I somehow lost my taste for the game, probably because of the crowded conditions of the municipal links, and my clubs have been rusting in the garage for years, in neglected disuse.

Anyone for tennis? Here was another form of athletics in which I had no formal training, but which I learned to play well enough so that I got a lot of fun out of it. We lived just a few blocks from the Teachers College tennis courts, and hardly a day went by during the favorable weather periods, that I did not put them to use. Even if I had spent a full day caddying at the golf links, I would always enjoy a set or two after dinner before the sun set. I would get up early many a morning and play a few sets with my sister, Sally, who had to be at work in the bank by nine o'clock. I never got to be very good at the game, although I developed what I liked to think was a terrific cannonball serve. I would enter all of the municipal tournaments, and any time I managed to survive the first round I figured I was doing well.

It was really my sister Boots who was the athlete *par excellence* of our family. I'll never forget the year in which she won the coveted title of women's champion among all of the female tennis players in La Crosse. One after another she defeated Helen Stewart, Henrietta Harget, and other really excellent players. In the finals she met Wilda Hickish, Art Tausche's girl friend. She was a superb player, considered unbeatable by any of the local talent, and Art was arrogantly predicting it would be no contest. He inveigled me into a five-dollar bet on the match, for much as I loved my sister and earnestly hoped for her victory, deep in my heart I didn't give her much chance. But I couldn't let that cocksure Art Tausche know this, so I backed her with my hard-earned cash. It was a hard-fought match, very even all the way, and when Boots emerged victorious, I could hardly believe it. This happened during the days when Helen Wills was at the height of her game. Boots wore a sun-visor during these matches which gave her a slight resemblance to Miss Wills, so from that time on we called her "Little Miss Pokerface."

That evening I worked as doorman at the Majestic Theater, with Boots as one of the ushers. Unknown to Boots, we typed out a special slide which read:

> THE USHER IN THE CENTER AISLE,
> MISS BERTHA VOLKOFF,
> THIS AFTERNOON BECAME
> THE WOMEN'S TENNIS CHAMPION
> OF LA CROSSE.
> LET'S GIVE HER A HAND.

Then we framed it so that just before the picture started, with the theater pretty well-filled with patrons, Boots ushered a couple down to the very front row. Just as she turned to walk back to the rear of the theater, the slide was flashed on the screen, the operator played a spotlight on her, and the audience burst into applause as she returned to her post in blushing embarrassment. Afterwards, we all had a surprise party for her at which she was presented with a new visor and a box containing half a dozen tennis balls. It was a thrilling day for her, one which she'll never forget. Marty Marks, who eventually became her husband, confided in me that what really made him fall in love with her was the fact that she was so good at sports but still kept her feminine charm.

As far as track and field-type sports are concerned, there is only one thing that stands out in my memory. I was never a fast runner, so I am still mystified at what happened the day our gym class at the Teachers College held a relay race, each man running about a quarter of a mile. I was third man in our particular group, and when I was handed the baton I was a good ten yards ahead of my competitor, who happened to be about the fastest runner in the class. I ran as though the devil himself were behind me, expecting any moment to see him go whizzing by, leaving me far behind. But he never gained on me! Whether he wasn't feeling well that day, or whether, knowing he was such a fast man gave me added impetus, I was still ten yards ahead of him at the finish of that quarter-mile leg. Maybe I just over-rated him—maybe I under-rated myself, I don't know, but I was the most surprised and pleased members of that gym class that day. It was by far my best effort as a runner.

As to spectator sports, I first became a baseball fan one bright April afternoon when I was in the sixth grade. Our principal, Mr. Kircher, had declared a half-day holiday for the benefit of any of the boys and girls who desired to go to the opening day of the baseball season, to which we children were admitted free of charge. La Crosse had a team which was in a league which was in a league composed of teams from other cities throughout the state and, inasmuch as one of the La

Crosse pitchers, "Cutz" Fitzie, lived just around the corner from out home, I was a made to order fan for the club. Through the years I became a loyal follower of the fortunes of the La Crosse team and rarely missed a game if I could help it, especially when lanky Larry Schaeffer, our next-door neighbor won the berth of second baseman on the team, and, although not a homerun hitter, would regularly rattle the fences for lengthy doubles.

These were the years that the bearded House of David baseball team went barnstorming across the country and annually made La Crosse one of their ports-of-call. After the regular baseball season was over, we were always visited by one or two pickup "all-star" teams, composed of players from the National and American Leagues. These were fun, but the most exciting teams to watch were the Negro aggregations who combined a great sense of comedy with flawless performances, much as the Harlem Globetrotters do in basketball today. There was one pitcher—I'm not absolutely sure, but it couldn't have been anybody else but the immortal "Satchel" Paige, who would load the bases on purpose with nobody out, call in both his outfield and infield, and with just the pitcher and catcher working, calmly proceed to strike out the side. My interest in baseball continued throughout my adult life. I followed the Memphis "Chicks" during my five years in Memphis, and was a loyal adherent of the Hollywood Stars until their dissolution last year when the Dodgers brought big league baseball to Los Angeles.

If I, together with the La Crosse citizenry, held an active interest in baseball, we were mad about football. I acquired the football fever early in life. While I was in grade school there were several Jewish boys on the high school football team who were my idols. We lived within a half-mile of the fairgrounds, in the center of which was the football gridiron. On the day of a game, we could plainly hear the roar of the crowd from our home, and if, perchance, dad had decided that on this particular day I was to stay home and rake the leaves or split some firewood, I was the most woebegone boy in town. Usually he would note the situation and wave me off with a smile, at which I would scamper for the fairgrounds as fast as my legs would carry me.

At that time there were no dressing rooms at the fairgrounds, so the teams would usually get into their uniforms in the Teachers College locker room a few blocks away, then walk over to the gridiron. I would wait about a block away from the gate, and when I saw the team approaching would run over and grab part of the gear of one of the Feinberg boys, or of Oscar Tobias, and with their arms protectively around me, would march proudly through the gate as the gate attendant conveniently looked the other way. If I arrived too late for this procedure it was still easy to sneak in by racing around to the far end of the circular track which surrounded the gridiron, then, while the guards were busily chasing other kids intent on the same purpose, quickly hurdle the low fence in back of the track and high-tail it for the grandstand to lose ourselves in the crowd.

La Crosse was really a rabid football town. The high school teams, especially in the days when I went to high school, were loaded with talent, and we were always in contention for the state championship. The Friday nights before a Saturday state championship game were really nights to remember. They usually started off early with a giant pep rally in the high school auditorium. I don't know whether high schools these days have the fantastic yells which were concocted for us, but we really had some honeys. Things like:

> *Strawberry shortcake, huckleberry pie,*
> *V-I-C-T-O-R-Y.*
> *Will we win? Well, I guess!*
> *La Crosse High School, Yes, Yes, Yes!*

> *Vee, Vee, Vee! Vee, vie, vum!*
> *Vee, vie, Vee, vie, Vee, vie, vum!*
> *Rat trap, cat trap, quicker than a steel trap,*
> *Cannibal, cannibal, Ziss, Boom Bah!*
> *La Crosse High School, Rah, Rah, Rah!*

> *Racheta boom! Racheta boom!*
> *Racheta, Racheta, Boom, Boom, Boom!*
> *Ripper Rah, Ripper Ree,*
> *La Crosse High School, Yes Sireeeee!*

Together with the standards, such as "Give 'em the axe," and the "Old Locomotive," coupled with a few stirring fight songs, the cheer leaders had plenty of ammunition to egg their cohorts into a frenzy. This indoor mass pep meeting was then broken up in favor of a huge campus bonfire around which we snake-danced, and in front of which the football coach and our heroes were introduced, only to be trundled off to bed early while we lined up for our big parade throughout the downtown section. These parades were noisy affairs, filled with happy, laughing, boisterous snake-dancing groups, setting many a trolley car off schedule by disconnecting them from their overhead wire contacts, and finishing up invariably by rushing one of the downtown theaters. The theater management was very cooperative, asking only that the students conduct themselves like ladies and gentleman and commit no acts of vandalism. We would usually line up in front of the theater and wait until the end of the first show when we were allowed in. Before the second show began, cheerleaders would appear on stage and lead the crowded house through a repertoire of yells and songs. Then everybody would settle down, watch the picture, go home to bed and dream about victory for the morrow.

When I went to the Teachers College, I satisfied my athletic instincts by acting as sports editor for our weekly school newspaper, The Raquet, in which I also wrote a weekly sports column, "**Seen From the Sidelines**, by Joe". During this period I bummed my way to Chicago to cover a football game, but that's a different story which I shall cover in a subsequent chapter.

ODD JOBS
1921-1926
(AGE 15-20)

I have held down a lot of odd jobs during my teen-age years, but perhaps the oddest or most unique one of which I can safely say no other man can lay claim, was part of my over-all job while working for the La Crosse Theaters Company.

The Rivoli theater boasted an organist who was without equal in his ability to "make the mighty Wurlitzer talk." Furthermore, the man was blind! Walter Goetzinger had for years been the town's leading organist, and his overtures before the curtain went up on the evening's entertainment were alone worth the price of admission. Before talkies made their debut in 1927, Walter played the Rivoli and sometimes the Majestic Theaters. It was my job to "read" the picture to him, so that he could arrange and map out his musical score. We would choose some morning for a special screening before the picture was scheduled to open. As the picture unfolded, I would describe the action to Walter as best I could, and at each change of scene, would insert a little metal plug in an electrical device installed near the organ, which would buzz at the proper time, informing Mr. Goetzinger that here was a spot for a change in music. He had a remarkable memory, and after one reading would make no mistakes as to the correct music for each ensuing scene. That was truly an "odd" job for a growing lad.

Another odd job which involved my work for the La Crosse Theaters Company, one which I enjoyed immensely, concerned the Guy and Eloda Beach Stock Company, an organization which played La Crosse for several months each year with great success in the 1920's. Guy would let me play bits in some of his super productions, and I was overjoyed when he assigned me a role in one of the great successes of the era, *Rain*. As the native chieftain of Pango-Pango, I found on the beach the body of one of the principals who had committed suicide. Resplendent in my body make-up (I was naked to the waist), I came rushing on stage yelling excitedly, "Yun kie kay! Yun kie kay! Filo keepee manoovi, kee kah wee awahnah, oh, lah nah tah, doc two!!" Now, I have been in a number of plays in my time, and for the life of me, I can't remember a line from any of them. But this bit of meaningless gibberish has clung in my memory for some thirty-five years. Is there a psychiatrist in the house?

Another off-beat type of work in which I engaged in my teens, something which could still be done to advantage today, human nature being what it is, was a job in which I was employed by the La Crosse Public Library. My duties were to collect overdue books, books which were so long overdue that there was little hope left for their return. I was paid so much a book for every one I could pick up, and it was really surprising the number of books I would accumulate during the course of a day. They usually gave me a list of books which had been overdue six months or more, and after several hours the wire basket on my bicycle would be overflowing. It proved to me that people were inherently honest—that the fact that they failed to return the books was due to carelessness, forgetfulness, and irresponsibility. Usually, they had actually forgotten that they still had the book and were sure that they had returned it months ago, but if I could get their permission to rummage among their bookshelves, I could usually come up with it, to their complete astonishment. This means of earning a livelihood might still prove to be a novel and profitable means for some enterprising young man of today to work his way through school.

One of my earliest methods of earning a little extra spending money was by means of the snow shovel. After each snowfall I would don mittens, galoshes, and overcoat or sweater, and, depending on the thermometer, sally forth to shovel snow at anywhere from fifty cents to two dollars a walk, depending on the size of the walk and the depth of the snow. It was during one of these early expeditions that I met the meanest man in the world. He must have been sixteen or seventeen. I was eight. He had just started shoveling the walk of a large corner house. A double-walk job which must have netted him at least two dollars. He offered me fifty cents if I would help him, to which I agreed. So, while he sat on his keester, smoking one cigarette after another, I dug in and did the whole job practically single-handed. He collected for the whole job, told me he'd pay me my share tomorrow, and started off. I told him I wanted my share now, but he pushed me into a snow bank and ran. That was the meanest, dirtiest deal with which I ever had to contend. I wish I could write a happy ending to this episode, but he did get away with it, and since then I have never been fully convinced that crime doesn't pay!

Other winter-type jobs included brief forays into the selling of Sunday newspapers. These were the Chicago papers which came in early Sunday morning by train, and were distributed by those enterprising Levy brothers. I had a paper route for a few Sundays, but this was too hard on dad, who, eager to help me off to a good start, would arise at three o'clock in the morning with me. With the help of our faithful old dobbin, King, he would assist me in making deliveries in weather way below zero or during raging snowstorms. When I gave that up, I tried selling Sunday morning papers in the downtown area, but wasn't too successful. I guess I just wasn't cut out for the newspaper game. My summers, of course, were devoted to the golf links, but each summer I would try my hand at some job or other, none of which would last more than a week.

One summer I hired out as a strawberry picker at L Crescent Farm, just across the Mississippi River, at five cents a box and all the berries I could eat. Within a week I broke out in a rash from eating too many berries, and was back at my cad-dying chores.

The next year I got a job at a local ice cream plant working on a delivery truck tamping down ice around the ice cream container with a baseball bat, a job which meant hard work practically every minute of the day. I lost interest in less than a week, and it was back to golf links.

Perhaps the shortest job I ever held in my life lasted from eight A.M. to noon of the same day. I was working in a bakery, and my duties consisted of shifting half-baked loaves of bread from one spot to another in large revolving ovens. As I opened the ovens to shift the loaves, hot blasts of sweetish, dry air would assail me until I became nauseous and told the foreman I was just physically unable to con-tinue. I wasn't actually fired, but undoubtedly would have been had I not quit just before the noon whistle blew.

During the summer of 1922, just before my senior year in high school, together with a lot of other football hopefuls, I worked as a railroad section hand, in an effort to tone up my body for the coming football season. We worked bare to the waist under a broiling sun, putting in ties, replacing old rails, and laying roadbeds, but instead of hardened muscles, all I got was a terrifically sunburned back. I will say that I stuck it out all summer, and was a more healthful lad for the experience, though I didn't make the football team.

When I was fourteen, I started working for the La Crosse Theaters Company, and kept this job (off and on, after school, evenings, and week-ends) until I left La Crosse in 1928. Besides reading the silent movies for the blind organist, doing bits for the Guy Beach Stock Company, I did practically everything there was to be done around a theater. I ushered, acted as doorman, changed signs, distributed advertising material, fired the furnace in the winter time, participated in promo-tional stunts, wrote advertising copy; in fact, actually apprenticed myself for a job as a theater manager, which I probably would have ended up doing, had it not been for a noisy, static-laden brat called R-A-D-I-O, which was just beginning to make itself heard along about 1927. But more about that in a later chapter.

Tom Thumb
1930
(Age 24)

Miniature golf, an outgrowth of the Depression, was a means of inexpensive entertainment for the entire family. Its popularity soared like a rocket during 1923 to 1930, then plummeted just as rapidly. By 1931 the craze had run its course and was already part of the history of the times.

I was in Pasadena, California, during the latter part of 1923 when I first noticed these miniature courses which had mushroomed in every vacant lot, all of which were doing an excellent business. The more I saw of them, the more the idea obsessed me that if they could make money in Southern California, there was no reason why they couldn't be successful back in La Crosse, Wisconsin. I talked to representatives of the Tom Thumb Company, who originated the whole idea, and whose Tom Thumb courses were considered the best of the various types then in operation, and found that it would take about five thousand dollars to swing a deal for a nine hole course, including installation. I was not a promoter, but I was sold on the profit-making possibilities of miniature golf, considered it more than a passing fad, and thought there was a good possibility of interesting somebody to back me financially in the project.

So, in the spring of 1930, I returned to the town of my birth to plunge into the one and only business venture of my life, a venture which proved eventually to be a fiasco, but which was fun while it lasted. One more season and we would have had it made, but I'm getting ahead of my story.

The first thing I did upon my arrival at La Crosse, was to contact a friend of mine, Ted Smith, a golfing pro at the La Crosse Country Club. Ted listened to my pitch, seemed interested, and asked me to take it easy while he contacted friends of his who might be interested. The idea appealed to Ed Erickson, a club member who ran a successful bakery. I was able to raise about five hundred dollars, Ted invested fifteen hundred, with Erickson making the major investment of three thousand dollars. We took a long-term lease on an empty lot on Fifth Street, just a block from Main Street, an ideal location on the fringes of the downtown sector. I wired the Tom Thumb people to start installation, we incorporated, I was to act as manager at twenty-five dollars a week, and we were in business.

All of these pre-construction negotiations and various unforeseen crises which arose took time, so we didn't have our formal opening until July 4Th. Things really looked rosy during those first few summer months. At a twenty-five cent fee for the nine holes, we would gross anywhere from one hundred fifty to two hundred dollars daily. Our major expenses were the lights. As we stayed open until midnight, we needed a lot of flood lights to keep the course well brightened during the evening hours, and those hours of abundant electricity ate into our profits. Then, of course, there was the monthly rental, my salary, and, inasmuch as we were open from nine a.m. until midnight, I had my sisters, and Boots, plus Helen Stewart, working for me in shifts; also, a couple of boys to keep rolling the greens which were made up of cotton seed dyed green to resemble grass.

We held a number of promotional stunts to keep up interest. An exhibition match between Ted Smith, who represented La Crosse as a professional golfer, and a visiting pro from nearby Winona, Minnesota, was advertised over the radio and in the newspaper, and drew a tremendous crowd. Monthly tournaments for both men and women were conducted, with loving-cups and plaques to the winners. The finals of one tournament match between two teenage girls almost resulted in a hair pulling contest, each one accusing the other of cheating. Poor old me, attempting to act with the wisdom of Solomon, canceled the match, and then walked around with them, score card and pencil in hand, as they replayed it, with the loser still insisting she was robbed.

Mother and dad were really very proud of me during those hectic days. They would come down to the course, stand just outside the fence, and just beam as they saw the crowds wait in line for their turn (as the supply of putters gave out). Their son had somehow become a successful business tycoon—just how they weren't sure, but there were the crowds to prove it.

Tom Thumb also acted as Cupid, for it was here, while my sister was acting as cashier one evening, that she was spotted by Joe Zovar, who wheedled an introduction out of me. That night he gave Rose and my mother a ride home, and those rides soon grew into a regular procedure until they at last led to the altar.

One never knows how he will react in a crisis. I am not a brave man; I am usually sensible and far from foolhardy. However, in one experience I had during this period I reacted neither sensibly nor sanely.

Each night after locking up about midnight, I would put the day's receipts in a bag furnished me by my bank, walk several blocks to the bank's outside deposit box, open it with a key furnished me for the purpose, and slide the bag containing the money down the chute where it would be safe until I came to check my deposit the next day.

One Saturday night, after a particularly good day of business, I took the day's receipts (well over three hundred dollars) to the bank as usual. Just as I turned the key opening the vault, a car pulled up to the curb and a harsh voice commanded, "All right, put 'em up! This is a stick-up!"

My first reaction was to save the money. I quickly opened the door of the depository, shoved the bag down the chute beyond the reach of the bandit, then turned to face him. It was only then I realized how foolish this action had been. As it turned out, the holdup man was just a friend of mine, Bill Walter, playing a practical joke. But if this had been the real thing, I would probably have been shot down in cold blood by the frustrated gunman. Bravery? No, I would say stupidity would be a better word.

The months of July, August, and September were wonderful. Business held up during most of October, but then chilly weather had begun to set in, and by the time November rolled around we were ready to call it quits until the following spring. But we were delighted. If the next spring and summer business could just approximate that of the past few months, we knew that we could have it made. We weren't prepared for what happened.

The following spring, we had the course thoroughly gone over, various spots repainted, and were all set for a banner year. But, alas, instead of two hundred dollar days, we started to gross two and three dollar days. We couldn't understand it. Why would the very same people who had flocked to play just a few short months ago have lost all interest in the game for no reason at all? We didn't realize at the time that it was a national trend; that all over the country miniature golf courses were folding, that the fad was over, and that we could do nothing about it. Thus ended my career as a businessmen. Soon after we closed during the autumn of 1930, I entered the field of radio, which became my life…but that's another story, another chapter.

ME AND DEMON RUM

Some of my best friends are alcoholics! Most of them are arrested cases, thanks to Alcoholics Anonymous, although one or two are still fighting it. Never do I see a man, sodden and bestial under its demoralizing influence, but that I utter a silent prayer of gratitude—"There, but by the grace of God, go I."

Although never a heavy drinker, there was a period of my life that I was a steady drinker. During my five years in Memphis, Tennessee, scarcely a day went by that I didn't have something of an alcoholic nature to drink, mostly some concoction containing gin, a southern favorite, but thank the good Lord I never acquired a taste for it. Where some of my friends needed a drink or two to sober up the morning after the night before, a bit of the hair of the dog that bit them, the mere thought of a drink the morning after a drinking bout would make me nauseous. So it wasn't too much of a sacrifice, when I married a girl who was a teetotaler, to join her. It's been many years since I've tasted alcohol in any form, and if I never have an alcoholic drink again, I won't miss it.

Although my father was not a hard liquor man, our home was never without its wine, mostly home-made, sweet, concord grade, dandelion, or elderberry wine. Wine was a part of our religion, as every Friday night, before our Sabbath meal began, the wine glasses were filled as part of the ritual in which we thanked God who made the fruit of the grape.

I remember as a child being sent to the family entrance of the nearest saloon with a large bucket which the genial, florid-faced saloon keeper would fill with cold, foamy tap beer for about fifteen cents. This I would carefully carry home, trying not to spill a drop, and once home, would get my reward in the form of a large glassful of the sudsy brew, sweetened with a couple of spoonfuls of sugar. This I dearly loved, especially on a hot, sticky summer day.

I was thirteen when the Volstead Act brought prohibition to our fair land back in 1919. At first, this meant nothing to me, although I do remember some of my high school classmates who thought it was smart to come to school with hip flasks containing bootleg whiskey.

It wasn't until my college days that drinking held any interest for me. My cronies, Frank Schneider, Herb Ristow, Ed Horschalk, and Bill Welter were no juvenile delinquents. In fact, we were all considered paragons of virtue as far as adolescents of the day were concerned. None of us smoked; we had no interest in wild women; we were studious and hard working. But we did love to get into a car of a balmy summer's evening, roll along the countryside singing at the top of our voices, and stopping at every available tavern for a glass or two of beer which was readily available almost everywhere. Ed Horschalk's older brother ran a saloon which was one of our favorite stops, and even though the sale of intoxicating liquor was prohibited, we had no feeling that we were breaking the law, as beer was sold quite openly, and everyone who wanted a drink bought it quite as a matter of course. One Saturday night, Herby, Frank, Ed and I contributed to the delinquency of Sherman Crane, one of our schoolmates who had never had a drink of any kind of alcoholic liquor in his life, but who was curious to experience the sensations of which he had heard so much. We took him with us on our rounds of the taverns, plied him with beer, and put him on the train at midnight, bound for his home town, in high spirits, singing lustily, just as drunk as he could be. The next morning he was scheduled to conduct a Sunday-school class in his home town. That's the last time I ever saw Sherman, although I hear that he is now happily married and a successful school teacher.

Ed, Herby, Frank and I all worked for the La Crosse Theaters Company, and we would sometimes chip in to buy a couple of quarts of home-made bootleg wine which we would consume in the basement of the Majestic Theater during the course of an evening's ushering. If I were in any danger of developing into a skid-row wino, this danger was eradicated suddenly one Saturday night when, after imbibing the contents of one of these bottles of bathtub vintage wine, we discovered a dead cockroach in the dregs of that bottle. For years afterwards the very thought of wine made me nauseous.

During those hectic prohibition days, La Crosse was no better nor worse, I suppose, than hundreds of its small town counterparts throughout the country. It had its share of key clubs, of "speakeasies", of taverns. Liquor of all kinds was easily obtainable for those who wished it, and enforcement of the eighteenth amendment was half-hearted and ineffectual. As part owner and manager of a miniature golf course, and later as a semi-celebrity, a man in the public eye as a radio announcer, I considered myself something of a big shot, and held keys to several of the town's leading key clubs. These were merely speakeasies with locked doors which were easily opened by members who held keys. Each one of us thought he was one of a privileged few, but, in reality, almost anyone who desired a key was accepted as a member of the club. There was a big dance hall in north La Crosse which was literally surrounded by homes which had been converted into speakeasies. It was considered smart to walk your dancing partner to one of these living rooms between dances for refreshment. Even the nicest girls seemed to get a thrill out of visiting these forbidden spots, and most of them did a thriving business. (I'm referring, of course, to the speakeasies.)

Pure grain alcohol is mighty potent stuff. I found this out one Saturday night when I went stag to a dance accompanied only by a pint of pure alcohol, which I sipped through a straw from time to time during the evening. I went in stag, and came out staggering. It was one of the very few times in my life that I was really intoxicated. I remember leaving the dance, reeling out to the parking lot where, for about five hours, I fought to get the key of my car into the door handle so that I might open the car door. It was a most peculiar feeling to see that keyhole, reach out for it with the key in my hand, only to feel myself surging backward instead of forward, unable to come close to the keyhole. The door handle seemed to play tricks on me, to back away from me as though purposely attempting to evade me. Eventually I made it. I got into the car and mercifully passed out completely. This was a lucky break for me, for had I attempted to drive home in my sodden condition, I doubt that I would have made it. I must have opened the window of the car just before I passed out, for when I awoke several hours later, it had begun to rain, and I felt the cooling splashed on my face. By this time I had recovered sufficiently so that by slow and extremely careful driving, I was able to make my way home. I never told anyone of that experience and probably shouldn't mention it now, except that I feel in a True Confessions mood.

When I arrived in Memphis early in 1932 to take up my announcing duties at Station WMC, one of my first experiences the day I made my debut was to be invited to have a drink by my boss, Henry W. Slavick, manager of the station. My first reaction was to turn down the invitation, as I wasn't sure that I wasn't being tested as to whether or not I would drink while on duty. However, I soon found out that such was not the case, and that a day in the lives of most Memphians was considered lost if it did not include at least one gin ricky or its equivalent. I may be a bit unfair here, as one of the announcers on our staff, a fellow by the name of Roth, who also bore the appellation, "Doc Sunshine," was an ordained Baptist minister and, so far as I knew, completely abstained from imbibing alcoholic refreshments. John Gleghorn, also a staff announcer, was a non-imbiber, but, shall I say, the majority of my confreres were, to say the least, social drinkers. Although some bourbon and scotch was consumed, gin in its various combinations seemed to be the favorite drink "down south".

During my first three years in Memphis I lived in room 212, Hotel Gayoso, just around the corner and on the same floor on which the radio station was located. Some day, I intend to write a book about room 212, which might turn out to be very interesting, as many exciting events took place within its four walls. Room 212 was seldom locked. Even while I was on duty, my friends would use it as their headquarters for all sorts of escapades, and more than once I was almost thrown out of the hotel for wild parties which went on there of which I was unaware. Of course, there were some in which I did participate, such as the Saturday night we had a noisy roomful of revelers while on both sides of us and across the hall, rooms had been rented to a group of Baptist ministers who were having a convention in Memphis. After their first complaint to the management, we invited them in for a drink, an invitation which they indignantly turned down. After the third complaint, if it hadn't been for the fact that I was a personal friend of the house detective, we probably would have been thrown out. However, I tactfully suggested to my guests that we all go over to a famous barbecued rib spot where we could finish our evening with the tastiest barbecued ribs in town, which we did.

There was a group of pretty nurses from a small private hospital who would filch some grain alcohol from the hospital supply room and smuggle it up to my room. We would then order some cherry phosphates from the drugstore of the hotel, and our liquor problem was solved for the night. Although most of the parties we had were on the noisy side, they were on the whole, harmless and not the drunken orgies one might suppose. We would do a lot of singing, both as a group and individually, especially if some of the guests were musicians who had brought along their instruments. We would play games such as ten questions or charades, and sometimes everybody would relax while I read some favorite poems from selections which had proved popular from readings on the air.

One Sunday afternoon I was off duty and a group of my friends were, as usual, planning a party in my room. I had been rehearsing for a Little Theater play, the dress rehearsal of which was scheduled for that evening. I decided to play it smart and drink no hard liquor that afternoon. Instead, I bought a pint of what I thought was a very weak, orange sloe gin. This tasted so insipid that it had me fooled, and before the afternoon was over, I had consumed the entire pint by myself. Now, I'll not admit that I passed out from the drinks. I was, however, tired physically from the long hours which I had been keeping holding down my job plus the weeks of rehearsal for the play, and late in the afternoon I fell asleep. Nobody had the heart to awaken me and, as a result, I slept through the night and didn't awaken until the next morning. It was then that I called the director, Eugart Yerian, offered profuse apologies, and tried to explain to him what had happened. Good old reliable Joe! After that, when I wanted to be sure to be in top control of my faculties, I just didn't drink—period.

I once received a Christmas gift from one of Memphis' favorite radio characters, an Italian named Tony, "I hope you enjoy myself," :six half-gallon bottles of his homemade wine, and one half-gallon jug of his best homemade brandy. I put these in a corner of my closet, and when my Negro maid came in to clean the room the day before Christmas, I pointed out the bottles and told her she could have one of the bottles of wine as my Christmas gift to her. I took great pains to show her which was the brandy bottle and to let her know that was the one bottle she was <u>not</u> to touch. Then I left her to attend to my announcing duties. When I returned some hours later, the brandy bottle was missing, whereas all six wine bottles were still in their places.

The next day I confronted her, madder than a wet hen and ready to tell her off. However, she smiled ingratiatingly, looked me square in the eyes, and said blandly, "Mistuh DuVal, that wine you give me fo' Christmas was the bestest wine Ah ever did taste in mah life. It was really scrumptious." Well, what was I to do? The damage was done, the brandy was gone, and though I knew she had literally stolen it, there was no sense in raising a ruckus at this stage. I told her I was glad she liked it, wished her a merry Christmas, and that ended that.

My son, David, recently had occasion to see a man in the throes of alcoholism—sick, shivering, incoherent, unable to walk without staggering, a veritable derelict of humanity. He had seen this same man a week or so previously, without knowing of his affliction, and the man had impressed him as being intelligent, friendly, neat in appearance, hard-working, honest, with a winning personality.

"If ever I am tempted to take a drink," said Dave, "all I have to do is remember this poor fellow and what drink did to him, That's all the sermon against alcohol I need."

Joe, The Radio Announcer
1930
(Age 24)

During the late autumn of 1930, a group of us who had gone to the State Teachers' College together decided it might be fun to produce some one-act plays on WKBH, the La Crosse radio station. Radio in those days was still in its swaddling clothes. Station WKBH had been on the air for less than three years, and its programming consisted chiefly of recordings and remote dance hall broadcasts, Uncle Art with a daily children's hour, and an occasional sports broadcast. Dramatic shows were still a thing of the future, even for the networks, which were just getting organized.

We drew straws to determine who would approach Mr. Joseph Calloway, owner of the station, with the idea, and as luck would have it, I was selected to be our spokesman. Mr. Calloway was very cordial and receptive to the idea. Suddenly he asked me, "Joe, have you ever thought of becoming a radio announcer?"

The idea had never entered my mind. I had the notion that all radio announcers were master of ceremony types—glib, witty, and with a natural gift of gab. I told this to Mr. Calloway, and he said, "Did you know, Joe, that ninety percent of what you hear on the air is read from a piece of paper?" No, I hadn't realized that. It seems that I had come to Mr. Calloway at just the opportune time. Several days previously, the head announcer of the station had run off with another announcer's wife, the company car, and some money, and WKBH was in dire need of a man to replace him. Frankly, with the nip of winter already in the air, and my Tom Thumb golf course closed until spring, I had been looking around for something to do during the winter months. So when Mr. Calloway auditioned me, liked the sound of my voice, and offered me the munificent sum of fifteen dollars a week to be raised to twenty-five once I had proved my competence and ability, I accepted with alacrity.

The next week La Crosse was to play River Falls Teachers' College in its annual homecoming game, which was also scheduled to be broadcast So, bright and early Monday morning I walked into Mr. Calloway's office, told him what I thought of the football broadcast, that I had been sports editor of our school paper, that I had played some football myself, and that I would like the assignment of doing play-by-play on the homecoming game. Mr. Calloway smiled and said, "I know, Joe, that I'm not a very good sports announcer, but I had no one to do the job for me, so I did it myself." Was I embarrassed! The very first day I reported for work I had told the boss that he was no good! But he took it good naturedly, and said if I would like to broad-cast the game Saturday, the assignment was mine.

I was delighted. In my mind's eye I could picture myself reeling off pictures of exciting runs a La Graham MacNamee. All that week during my spare time, I typed reams of copy about the two teams, their personalities, their past struggles with each other. "Tubby" Keeler, coach of the La Crosse team, promised to send me one of his subs as a spotter, as did the coach of the River Falls team. I rounded up several local sports figures to interview between halves. I did everything possi-ble to insure an interesting broadcast.

We went on the air from the stadium at 1:30 with the opening kickoff sched-uled for two o'clock. Everything went swimmingly during the first half-hour. I had plenty of copy and was reading smoothly about the rivalry between the two schools, not realizing how swiftly the time was passing. Engrossed in my copy, I felt a tap on my shoulder, then saw Mr. Calloway's finger pointing towards the gridiron. The two teams were in position, and the game was about to begin. I looked about—nobody was in the broadcasting booth but Mr. Calloway and myself. Neither team had sent me their promised spotters. Furthermore, it was a bitterly cold day, and both teams were wearing sweat shirts over their jerseys, completely covering their identifying numbers, and I hadn't the faintest idea of who was who. I never came so close to walking off a job in my life. Luckily, I had the starting lineups on two sheets of paper in front of me, so I waded in. Things went fairly well until both teams started making wholesale substitutions. Then I was completely lost as to who was handling the ball or who was making the tack-les. I would pick names at random from the roster of the teams on the program and, so far as the radio listeners were concerned, I guess it made no difference, for how were they to know whether I was right or wrong? After the first quarter it wasn't too bad and my half-time guests did show up for their interviews. But alto-gether, it was a harrowing experience.

When I arrived after the game to receive the plaudits of my family, I found that no one had listened. My sister Florence and her boy friend, Harry Grinstein (whom she later married), had been sitting in the living room all afternoon and had not so much as turned on the radio—they weren't interested in football. My ego was thoroughly deflated. What's that old saying—"A prophet is without honor in his own country." But some of my friends did listen, said that I gave an interesting account of the game, but seemed biased in favor of the La Crosse team, which incidentally, lost the game.

The following weeks proved to be exiting and interesting. I was serving my apprenticeship in radio and gaining invaluable experience. Mr. Galloway allowed me to experiment with any new program ideas within reason. The first thing I did was to inaugurate a weekly dramatic half-hour in which we would adapt well-known one-act plays for radio. Helen Stewart and I did an old English one-acter called *The Man on the Curb*, about a man and his wife who were starving because they couldn't find any work. I remember the tag line of the play, "God, oh God, give us bread!" We changed the locale from England to America, the time from the early 1900's to the present Depression, and really made a timely tear jerker out of it, which elicited many calls of commendation.

I started a daily Poet's Corner, a fifteen minute program which gathered quite a following. I read poems with plenty of heart appeal such as *The House With Nobody In It*, many of Edgar Guest's poems such as *A Heap of Livin'*, tear-jerkers such as *Young Fellow, My Lad*, and exciting narrative poetry such as Alfred Noyes' *The Highwayman*. I received a lot of mail, mostly from old ladies who enclosed religious poetry which they wanted me to read. These were not only religious but most of them were sectarian which I couldn't read to a general audience.

A weekly sports half-hour was a favorite of mine in which I interviewed local athletic coaches, high school and college football and basketball personalities, the sports editor of the La Crosse Tribune and Leader Press, our one daily newspaper, and any visiting sports celebrities who might be in town.

Our feature program was a daily Farm and Home hour, presented each week day from noon to one o'clock, which featured a twelve piece orchestra and amateur guest performers who came from the surrounding countryside. One of these guests, a harmonica player, had just finished a number, and I was standing at the microphone with my back to him, reading a commercial. Suddenly, I heard a terrific noise in back of me, and turned just in time to see him fall into the drum section of the orchestra. He was an epileptic and was in the throes of an epileptic fit. I finished my commercial as best I could, motioned to the orchestra to go into their next number, and several of us carried the gentleman into the next room. We loosened his clothing, and he soon recovered his composure and wanted to know if he could go back and do another number. We thought it best to save his encore for some future occasion.

Helen Stewart and I had perhaps one of the very first of the popular Mr. and Mrs. type programs which proved so popular in later years. We presented a news program by pretending to be reading the daily newspaper to each other over our morning coffee, calling each other's attention to various items of interest. It proved to be a winner, and we kept it going for many months. We carried several transcribed programs, one of which was Cecil and Sally which later gained some sort of record for longevity.

My early conception of a radio announcer as a master of ceremonies type was justified when I was assigned to do remote broadcasts from various outlying ballrooms. Announcing dance bands was fun and gave me a glowing feeling of importance as I master of ceremonied before groups of young dance-lovers.

As the months went by, and that promised raise was not forthcoming, I grew impatient. Mr. Calloway claimed that, with the Depression in full swing, he wasn't making any money and couldn't afford to pay me more money. On the other hand, I felt that, Depression or no Depression, fifteen dollars a week was a miserable pittance for the amount of work I was doing. Besides announcing all types of programs, I was writing advertising copy and soliciting advertisers for new programs I would dream up. I felt that I was ready for bigger and better things, that I had had a year of priceless experience, but that it was time to move on. So after almost a year at WKBH, I resigned and headed for Minneapolis.

Volkoff Becomes Du Val
1932
(Age 27)

How does one start out with the typical Russian name of Volkoff and finish up with one of the most popular of French surnames—Du Val? In my case, it happened in this fashion.

After I left WKBH late in the summer of 1931, I went to Minneapolis where I lived with my sister Marion and her husband, Art Figen. During this period I auditioned as an announcer at a St. Paul radio station, KSTP, and was told that the next staff opening would be mine. For months I haunted this studio hoping that one of their announcers would break a leg, or be promoted to some network job in New York, but they all seemed happy with their work and held on to their jobs. In the meantime, early in 1932, my brother-in-law asked me if I would consider a job in Memphis, Tennessee. It seemed the Minnesota and Ontario Paper Company, for whom he worked in a responsible position, owned The Commercial Appeal, billed as "The South's Greatest Newspaper", but which was, nevertheless, a victim of the Depression and couldn't pay its paper bills to Art's company. The newspaper had, as its subsidiary, a radio station, WMC, and this station had an opening for an announcer. I was definitely interested, but before I made a final decision, decided to have a final talk with the manager of station KSTP.

He advised me to grab the job, as that much promised opening at KSTP was still problematic. With the nation in the throes of the Depression, everybody, including announcers, were grimly hanging on to their jobs. Then suddenly he said, "Joe, if you intend to make a career for yourself in radio, I strongly advise that you change your name, at least for professional purposes."

"Oh," I asked, "and just what's wrong with Volkoff?"

"In the first place," he replied, "the 'k' in Volkoff is altogether too hard sounding, too unpleasant to the eardrums, and the name itself is not easy to remember."

I had never given the matter a thought. "Do you have any suggestions?"

"I would say that for the sake of euphony, if you have a first name of two syllables, your surname should have but one, so why don't you lop off the last syllable of your name and call yourself Joseph Vol?"

The name 'Vol' didn't particularly appeal to me—it was neither fish nor fowl. "What if I decide to use a one syllable first name, say 'Joe'? Then I suppose I should have a two syllable surname. Right?"

"Right." His brows furrowed in thought for a moment, then, as he banged his fist on the desk for emphasis, he fairly shouted, "How would you like to become a Frenchman?"

"A Frenchman? What do you mean?"

"From now on your name is Joe Du Val—accent on the 'Val' one dot over the 'a'. "It's perfect. It flows, it's soft—no hard consonants—I'd use it if I were you. What do you think?"

"Joe Du Val—Your announcer has been Joe Du Val—Hmmm,…not bad.", I thought.

So that's how I became Joe Du Val. When I reached Memphis and reported to Henry Slavick, station manager at WMC, as Joe Du Val, I felt like a criminal attempting to evade the law, and momentarily expected the hard hand of a representative of law and order clapped on my shoulders with a stern, "Joseph Volkoff, we are extraditing you back to Wisconsin to stand trial for falsely assuming a name which is not yours."

However, I soon became accustomed to the new moniker and used it constantly, not only professionally, but legally. It wasn't until after my son was born that I had the name legally changed, and it is with somewhat of a feeling of guilt that I realize that, inasmuch as I am the only living male of the Volkoff tribe, I am the last of the Volkoffs.

WMC
PROGRAM NOTES AND PERSONALITIES
1932-1937
(AGE 26-31)

Radio station WMC, the voice of the south's greatest newspaper, the Memphis Commercial Appeal, was typical of hundreds of other network affiliated stations throughout the country. When I arrived in 1932, the station carried programs from both the red and the blue networks of the National Broadcasting Company—later the blue network branched off to become the American Broadcasting Company. Although we carried most of the leading network shows of the time, the Jack Benny Show, Amos and Andy, Ed Wynn, Eddie Cantor, Arch Obolers Lights Out, Walter Damrosch and the NBS Symphony Orchestra, Ben Bernie, to mention just a few, it was really the local programs which gave the station its individuality. This was before the days of the disc jockey, as hit recordings were sparse items, and our record library was rather meager. We did have a studio orchestra, however, which was used constantly in many combinations, from five piece jazz combos to fifty piece concert orchestras for some of our more ambitious programs. There was a good deal of fine talent in Memphis upon which we drew for soloists, both classical and popular, but these were also available to other Memphis stations. What gave WMC its unique distinctiveness, setting it apart from the average station and giving it a position as the town's most listened to radio station, were programs such as The Court of the Air, Mickey Mouse, The Wandering Troubadour, Chronicles of the Presidents, Rube Turnipseed and his Memphis Hillbillies, Uncle Joe Reads the Funnies, and other notable productions, each of which had its own large group of faithful followers.

Perhaps the most popular of the locally produced shows during the more than five years in which I worked at WMC was The Court of the Air, a daily half-hour show which was aired early each evening. Although its title sounds as though it were the forerunner of the rash of "Courtroom" shows which now seem to permeate Southern California television, WMC's "Court" was purely and simply, a comedy show, a group of jokes involving a judge, a sheriff, and a group of stock-type defendants on trial for doing incongruous crime, each case surrounded by a musical number and the inevitable commercials. I think the secret of the program's success was its seeming spontaneity, and the fact that the whole cast seemed to be having a good time. Written by Milton Simon, our production manager, a man with a great sense of comedy, he was also an adept performer as he played the role of the sheriff and doubled, in a high falsetto, the part of a female counterpart of Step'n Fetchit, a negress who was forever falling afoul of the law, a character which would have been a howl in any coast-to-coast comedy show. I announced the show, did the commercials, and played the role of the judge. One of our regular culprits was Luther "Red" Rountree, guitar player in the orchestra, who played the role of Silas Hicks, a rural character who was always getting into trouble. Red, a freckle-faced, redheaded Texan, was a big hit in this role, although he seemed to resent the fact that he was elected to portray this rube character, and took it as a personal affront. We finally persuaded him that he should be grateful that he had the happy faculty of being able to make people laugh, a gift which many a comedian would envy. Years later, when Red came to Hollywood, he capitalized on this talent when he played the nephew of Bob Burns for several years, twanging away on his guitar, and doing very well in television.

Tommy Thompson, a young fellow with a gift for mimicry and an ability to "sell" a song by assuming a sort of gravelly Negroid quality to his voice, was one of the Court regulars as Mose Green, a shiftless colored boy. Milt Simon would sometimes write parodies to such numbers as "The Man on the Flying Trapeze", giving each cast member (including the Judge) a solo chorus, which was about as close as I ever came to becoming a professional singer. There was a period that I announced a fifteen minute program of popular songs featuring a local thrush, Harriet Willhite. On each program we selected a number which we performed as a duet, but instead of singing my chorus, I recited the words as though it were a poem, which made for a nice novelty effect. I never did have a good singing voice.

Not long after assuming my duties as station announcer at WMC, I almost lost my job through no fault of my own. I was on duty one Sunday…

I Know It's Spinach

Although I am by no means a finicky eater, and usually relish anything my wife sets before me, I draw the line at one vegetable, spinach. I hate spinach! I detest spinach! I have a phobia against eating spinach. This stems back, not to my childhood days, but to an incident which took place some thirty-three years ago (Ed. as of 1965) when, as a young rookie radio announcer from Wisconsin, I was attempting to ingratiate myself with the listeners of radio station WMC at Memphis, Tennessee.

It was my first Sunday morning on duty back in the autumn of 1932. As a young Yankee who was invading the southern airways, I was especially anxious to create a good impression. At eleven o'clock the station presented an hour church service by remote control, direct from one of the Memphis churches. I made the necessary announcement and the shift from studio to church was perfectly executed by our engineering department.

Things went well for the first ten minutes or so when suddenly there was a sharp click, followed by a period of dead air. The inevitable line-break, the bugaboo of those early radio days, had again taken place. It was my duty to inform the listeners that, "Due to circumstances beyond our control, we are forced to leave the church services for a few brief moments", and would then fill in with appropriate music from the studio until the line-break had been repaired."

In those days, the announcer on duty handled the playing of the recordings. There was a turntable on my desk, and as I spoke into the microphone, I reached into a bin of recordings at my side, grabbed one at random, placed it on the turntable, smoothly set the needle down, and all was well—or so I thought. The "appropriate" music which I had so unthinkingly selected turned out to be an Irving Berlin hit tune of the day from the musical show, *Face the Music,* entitled I say it's Spinach." As the orchestra swept into the opening bars, I stepped into the control room to assist the engineer regain contact with the church. I was still naively unaware of my impending doom, as this was the first time I had heard this particular song.

Then the vocalist took over. I could scarcely believe my ears as I heard him swing into, "I say it's spinach, and the hell with it!" This, of course, was about as inappropriate first line of a lyric to be used as a fill-in for a religious program as Satan himself could conjure up. But this was only the beginning of my troubles. As I listened dumbfounded, almost paralyzed with utter consternation, I heard, "I know it's spinach and the hell with it…the hell with it…the hell with it…the hell with it…". The needle had stuck at the worst possible spot. I rushed madly back into the studio to change the disc, but, by this time, the damage had been done. The phones started jangling. My ears blistered as the outraged Tennessean worshippers berated me as a

Damn Yankee Atheist! "If this is your idea of a joke, you got a perverted sense of humor and should go back to Wisconsin where you belong!" My attempted explanations were in vain. To make matters worse, the station manager, my boss, had listened from his home, and it was only the testimony of the engineer on duty, who intervened on my behalf, which saved my job.

It was a long time before I was able to live down this black Sunday and regain the friendship and confidence of those Memphians who were tuned in to the station that morning. To this day, when my wife occasionally sets a dish of spinach before me, even though she cleverly disguises it under cream, or embellishes it with other vegetables, I am not fooled. Cajole me as she will, my reaction is still, "I say it's spinach, and the hell with it!"

I Meet My Love in a *Dump Heap*
1937
(Age 31)

During the closing months of 1937, a Cuban actor friend, Jose Perez, asked me if I were interested in doing a little theater play. There were a number of these little theater groups in and around the Hollywood area, offering little or no pay to the aspiring young actor, but presenting him with an opportunity to showcase his talents, and perhaps, oh heavenly thought, to be seen by some motion picture mogul and cast, as a result, in his latest picture. I had already appeared in one of these epics, a play called *The Clock Ticks*, written and produced by Paul Gerard Smith. a rather eminent gag writer of the day, who had ambitions to do a serious drama. *The Clock Ticks* was a story of prison life, with the ticking of the clock offering a suspense element as the passage of time brought closer and closer the impending execution of one of the principals. In most plays, in order to quicken the pace and make the lines live, actors are instructed to pick up their cues and let no time elapse between lines of dialogue. In this play, with time as a suspense element, it was decided to experiment in the other direction, and we were instructed to count anywhere from three to five seconds between lines. The idea may have had some merit, but it slowed the action of the play down to such an extent that audiences lost interest before we were well under way, and the play died a-borning.

Anyhow, I decided to investigate Jose's lead, and an interview was arranged with the director, Edward Goering. The play was a product of the Depression called *Dump Heap*. The authoress, Mary MacDougal Axelson, had one hit movie to her credit, *Life Begins*, was a very capable writer, and had a good play in *Dump Heap*.

When I called upon Mr. Goering to be interviewed for the character heavy of the play, Hodges, I was met by his secretary, a girl named Roslyn Aarons—thin, rather anemic-looking—whose main charm was a pair of large brown, soulful-looking eyes. Her expression seemed somewhat brooding and unhappy, but she did have a charming, wistful smile, and even a merry, tinkling laugh in her brighter moments. I think what really first attracted me to her was the way those deceptively serene eyes of hers would catch fire when she became angry which was quite often. I remember climbing the stairs leading to the studios on one occasion, only to catch a glimpse of her flying down the stairs, eyes blazing, muttering something to the effect of, "I'll fix him! Who does he think he is, anyhow!" She evidently took a couple of turns around the block to cool off, for ten minutes later she was back in the studio, calmly going about her duties as though nothing had happened.

I wish I could say that I fell madly head over heels in love with her after one glance at those dark limpid orbs, and she with me. It would have made nice reading, but such simply was not the case. I liked Roz, and she got along well with me, but we were just one of a group of twenty to thirty people connected with the show, and it was months before any romantic overtones were forthcoming. I remember meeting her parents when they came to see the play, getting into a discussion with her dad on chess, and later, jestingly asking Roz for a date so I could come to her home to play chess with her dad.

Edward Goering was the typical European type producer who believed in drilling his cast thoroughly before allowing them to appear before the public. *Dump Heap* rehearsals dragged on interminably, week after week, month after month, before a theater was leased and a starting day set. Goering was an impractical businessman, operated the whole venture on a shoestring, was forever in financial difficulties, but was withal, an excellent director and producer. He made his living expenses from teaching dramatic classes, and Roz operated in the dual capacity as one of his dramatic students and acting as his secretary. Actually, *Dump Heap* was deserving of a much better fate than was its lot at his hands. The set was starkly realistic and very effective. The cast was above average for a little theater group, and the play itself was well-written and a worthwhile, interesting drama. But Goering had neither the money nor the know-how to give the production adequate promotion, and the three hundred seat capacity Las Palmas Theater more often than not had a half dozen or so paid admissions. It's a dismal experience for actors to play to an empty theater night after night. It wasn't long before *Dump Heap* was another little theater memory.

It was many weeks after the close of the play that quite by accident Roz and I met again. I was doing a radio show at KHJ, which was then still located on Bixel Street in downtown Los Angeles. During a rehearsal break I noticed her sitting in the outer office where she was awaiting an appointment to discuss the sale of some scripts written by her sister, Harriet. We were delighted to see each other, especially under such professional circumstances—I actually working for money, and she about to sell some dramatic scripts to the radio industry. Before I went back into rehearsal, I had made a date to visit her the next evening, presumably for the purpose of discussing the merits of sister Harriet's scripts. That, it turned out, was the beginning of the end.

I could easily have queered my chances with Roz completely early on that evening of that first date. As she wasn't quite ready to see me when I arrived, I was ushered into the living room, where her dad was listening to a radio address by the then Secretary of State, Cordell Hull. Mr. Aarons was a man of definite and violent likes and dislikes. Cordell Hull was to him a demigod who could do no wrong, one of the greatest men of his or any other century. Had I uttered one word of criticism against this man, I have no doubt but that I would have been thrown out on my ear. Luckily, I too had a very deep respect for Mr. Roosevelt's Secretary of State, and so informed Sam Aarons, so I had passed my first test. The evening proved to be a great success, although I confess we didn't spend much time discussing sister Harriet's radio scripts.

Then followed some wonderful get-acquainted sessions. I was still living with my sister Marion at the time, who generously allowed me to borrow the Figen family Buick for my dates. Roz and I would drive down to the beach and talk for hours. I would tell her of my Memphis adventures and misadventures, of Fran and Syl and other of my "southern flames", while she would regale me with stories of her cowboy, of her neurotic "Pat", whom she almost married, of her life as a roving magazine solicitor, and as a budding young actress at the Pasadena Playhouse. We found that we had missed each other by about a year at Pasadena.

My love for Roslyn got its real test when Marion and Art moved back to Minneapolis, and I had to make my way by bus and streetcar approximately ten miles from my rooming house to her home at the Shawnell Apartments, all this during the rainiest part of the year, the winter of 1938-39. It wasn't so bad getting there early in the evening or late afternoon, but sometimes, getting home in the rain about three o'clock in the morning posed quite a problem.

One Sunday afternoon, I was at my sister Sally's at Ocean Park, lazily enjoying the antics of Charley McCarthy and W.C. Fields over the NBC station KFI, when the phone rang. It was for me. Roz's terrified voice greeted me with some incoherent babbling about an invasion from Mars. I should hurry up and pack! We've got to get out of here. New Jersey had already capitulated, and the Martians were on their way to the West Coast! She had heard it all on the CBS news. Her father had already warned the other tenants of the Shawnell Apartments, and was even now packing what few belongings he could get together and was preparing to evacuate his family—although just where they would go to escape the clutches of the invading Martians was still problematic! I was the first one Roz thought of as the horrifying news came crackling through! If we had to die, we'd die together!!!

I remembered vaguely reading somewhere earlier that week that Orson Welles and his troupe of thespians was to present a dramatized account of a Martian invasion, and besides, why was NBC wasting its time with Charley McCarthy if an invasion was actually under way.

"Look, darling," I spoke in my most reassuring manner. "If we are actually being invaded by Martians, I don't believe that CBS would have an exclusive story on it. Now, I'll hold the phone. You go back to your radio, and if you can find any other station besides KNX that is carrying this story, let me know, and I'll be right over."

A few minutes later she came back and rather shamefacedly admitted that no other station seemed to have any inkling of the invasion except KNX. I then told her of the Orson Welles pre-program publicity which I had read, and she admitted that she had perhaps jumped at conclusions. And that's how I single-handedly saved my love from the Martians. In justice to Roz and her family, I must say that Orson Welles sent half the nation into a tizzy with this realistic broadcast, done in the form of news reports with no explanation that it was fiction. People all over the country were panic-stricken and ready to flee before the advance of the much feared Martians.

If the way to a man's heart is truly through his stomach, Roz used the right combination. She was always feeding me. There was a period early in our courtship in which my funds were so low that I found it expedient to purchase three pounds of seedless grapes for a dime, a diet upon which I subsisted for several days. So, when Roz extended one of her frequent dinner invitations either with her family or just the two of us in her apartment, I was usually only too happy to accept.

One delightfully charming dinner I shall always remember, consisted of roast wild duck, served with the compliments of her friend, Paquita Machris, who, with her husband, Maury, were avid hunters, and always bagged their full quota during duck season. Roz invited Jose Perez and me to this gourmand's delight, we pooled our resources to bring along a bottle of the best wine we could afford and really enjoyed a tasty, well prepared, candle-lit, out-of-the ordinary dinner. Jose was lavish in his praise of my girl, agreed that she was way above average in looks, intelligence, and ability to make wild duck a gastronomic thing of beauty, that she exuded real class, and that I would be an idiot if I didn't marry the girl. Who wants to be an idiot? So I married the girl.

We decided on March 16, 1939, for our wedding date as a sentimental gesture towards Roz's parents as this was the date of their wedding anniversary.

We had a quiet wedding with just members of the immediate families and a few close friends in attendance. Harriet loaned us her car for our honeymoon trip, and we set off that afternoon, with no definite plans, for a week's honeymoon. We had an early dinner at Eaton's Chicken Restaurant on La Cienega, where Roz embarrassed me by telling the waitresses that we were newlyweds. We bought a lot of extra fried chicken pieces which we took along and really enjoyed as picnic snacks during the next few days.

We spent our first night at a motel where we were kept awake most of the night by intermittent roaring sounds which sounded as though we were encamped in the midst of a jungle. The next morning we learned that our motel was located just in front of Gay's Lion Farm, and the roarings we heard during the night actually were lions. There are worse things in life, however, than to be kept awake on the first night of one's married life.

Of course, we had to visit Rancho Bella Vista, located in Corona, ten or twelve miles from Riverside, which had once belonged to her dad, and where Roz had spent several years of her life. It was a lovely spot, but Roz was dismayed when she saw that the new owners had cut down some of her favorite trees and made other changes which she considered pure sacrilege.

Then, over to Pomona where the National Orange Show was being held, and where Roz shamed me into taking a ride on the Ferris wheel, my first trip on any type of fun ride since that ill-fated ride on The Whip during the La Crosse County Fair during my boyhood. Then a drive through the mountain area to a vacation spot near Kern Camp, my first contact with snow in Southern California.

We took our time, had a glorious honeymoon vacation, and returned home to our little apartment on Eleanor Avenue just in time to accept a wedding gift from Frank Woodruff in the form of a call for Lux show.

Oh yes, that apartment—For several weeks before we got married, Roz and I trudged the streets of Hollywood searching for a place to live. We wanted something not too expensive, within walking distance of NBC and CBS, or at least close enough to a streetcar or bus line to get me there conveniently, as I had no car. There was always something wrong—either the rent was too high, the apartment was too dark, the neighborhood was too shabby, we just couldn't seem to find what we wanted. Once we thought we had it and were about to make a deal when the landlady added to her sales talk, "I'm sure you'll be glad to know that the vibrations here are wonderful!" The vibrations? What sort of weird cult did she belong to? We decided not to investigate further.

Finally, we found what we wanted, a light, clean, airy, moderately priced apartment located on Eleanor Avenue, a block south of Santa Monica Boulevard and a block East of Vine Street. It was within easy walking distance of Hollywood and Vine, and was the answer to our prayers.

We came home from our honeymoon just in time to surprise the apartment manager and her husband plus a couple of their friends giving our apartment an admiring inspection. We couldn't blame them, however. With their permission, Paquita had decorated our apartment with streamers, with nonsensical quotations, with good luck pieces, and various surprise doodads to greet us in our return. As they didn't expect us back quite as soon as this, they felt very foolish at being caught red-handed taking it easy in our apartment. However, we forgave them, and got quite a kick out of Paquita's ingenious decorations.

So ended my life of single blessedness, and thus began a period of life in double harness, sometimes smooth, sometimes rough, but withal a richly rewarding period of growth, of mutual love and affection which brought with it many of the happiest moments of my life and in which we will, come next Monday, have spent our twentieth year together.

HOW I HELPED WIN THE WAR
OR
MY LIFE AS AN ELECTRICIAN

The probability that I will ever reach the devoutly to be wished status of grandfatherhood is, at the moment, rather remote. My only child, a son of some twenty years, is at present unmarried and without any immediate prospects of matrimony. However, in the natural course of human events, I fully expect that eventually the time will come when a grandchild of mine, returning from a class in twentieth century history, will pipe up with, "Grandpa, what did you do to help win the war?"

I could tell him, sincerely and truthfully, that if he referred to World War I, I was twelve years old when the armistice was signed in 1918, that the extent of my war effort was keeping the weeds out of my victory garden, plus the unalloyed pride and joy I experienced caddying for members of the armed forces who preferred to spend their furloughs on the golf course.

I could honestly tell my grandchild that, if he referred to World War II, I was thirty-five, married, and a father when the unpleasantness began, and, what was more important, my draft board rated me as a big, fat 4-F, which meant that my worth as a fighting man to the army, navy, or marines, was practically nil.

However, I doubt whether I'll mention any of this when my grandchild comes to me with the inevitable question. Why should I, when I can look him straight in the eye and tell him, "Son, I helped Uncle Sam rebuild his fleet after it was practically destroyed at Pearl Harbor!!" Then, with head held high, I would recount my days of glory as maintenance electrician on the graveyard shift at Western Pipe and Steel, the Long Beach, California shipyards. I would skip the fact that my only qualifications as an electrician were the fifty dollars I had available, which enabled me to join the electricians' union, a necessary prerogative to securing employment in that field.

If you promise not to tell my grandchildren, I'll confess now that I was what was more of less affectionately known as a "shoe clerk" by the legitimate electricians at the shipyards. All I really knew about the electrician's trade was that, if I were smart, I'd stay away from the hot stuff, the high voltage electrical units.

The electricians were divided into teams of a half a dozen or so each, which were stationed strategically throughout various sections of the huge, sprawling shipyards. The group to which I was assigned consisted of two qualified electricians, master craftsman who knew their business, and four "shoe clerks". Actually, the bona fide electricians in our group did not resent the presence of those of us who were hoaxes. In fact, we made their life easier. One did not really have to be a legitimate electrician in order to perform adequately the duties of a mainte-nance electrician. Our job when we arrived on duty at midnight, the beginning of the graveyard shift, was to supply adequate lighting for the welders, the riveters, or any other working crews on duty during our shift. This meant little more than plugging in flood lamps, or drop cords, whatever the occasion demanded. Within a half hour, our job was usually completed. We had nothing more to do for the rest of the night, unless an emergency arose or some spot job was started which needed lighting. At dawn, we made the rounds of our section, gathered the drops and the floods, deposited them neatly in the proper spot, and awaited the eight o'clock whistle which proclaimed the end of our shift. We "shoe clerks" did ninety percent of the actual maintenance work, and really earned our wages. The two real electricians in our crew were paid, not for what they did, but for what they knew. They were used only in case of emergency or if a job came up which needed the know-how of a real electrician. Most of the time they let us do the run-of-the-mill maintenance work, while they studied their racing forms or caught up on their sleep. It was tacitly agreed upon that we do the drudgery while they performed the really important jobs which did come up from time to time. This arrangement worked very well, although it almost ended in complete disas-ter for me on one unforgettable evening.

It was an unusually busy evening. I had just returned to the electricians' shack after lighting up a section for a group of welders. I was the only man in the shack when there came a sharp rap at the door. As I opened the door, I was confronted by an agitated white-collar worker.

"Thank God you're back," he panted. "We need an electrician right away. Our lights have gone out!" As he talked, he pointed to a rather large two-story struc-ture about half a block away. It was a building used for paper work of various kinds in which a crew of twenty or thirty workers were employed. I saw at once that the building was indeed in stark, complete, abject, gloomy, darkness. I knew I was beyond my depth, and looked around frantically for someone to save me. Where were those two lazy, good-for-nothing electricians who were supposed to handle situations such as this? Earlier in the evening I had heard talk of an impending poker game at another electricians' shack about a half mile away, but I had no time to start searching for them. The office workers needed light and needed it fast. Besides, I just couldn't tell this young fellow who depended upon me to wait until I found an electrician. After all, wasn't I wearing the white hel-met with the red streaks of lightning zigzagged on the front of it?

With dragging feet, I shuffled irresolutely towards the darkened building, hoping against hope that I would at least encounter one of my fellow "shoe clerks". It was like trying to find a taxi on a rainy night—not a white helmet was to be seen in any direction. Although my mind was spinning furiously, I hadn't the faintest idea of what might have caused the blackout. I had the presence of mind to gather some spare fuses from a drawer in the electrician's shack, but I had no notion of where the fuse box of the building was located.

As we neared the building, I almost stumbled over a rather thick, dark, rubber-insulated cord. I vaguely followed the length of the cord with my eyes and noticed that it emerged from underneath the building and snaked its way to a J-box about a hundred yards away. Now, a J-box is a box containing eight or ten or twelve electrical outlets, half of which are on the right side of the box, half on the left.

An idea flashed into my non-electrical mind, an idea sparked by a bit of information I vaguely remembered from listening to several electricians random talk a few nights earlier. "Sometimes," I remembered hearing one of the electricians say, "half of the J-box is still in good working order." Inspired by this bit of electrology, which might yet mean my salvation, my unenthusiastic, ambling gait changed to an eager stride, as I almost ran to the J-box. With an air of authority and show of confidence which belied my real feelings, (I had to keep up appearances as by this time a group of the office workers had gathered round to watch me work) I pulled the plug of the cord from the outlet to which it was fastened. I could have tested it immediately by jamming it into one of the outlets opposite to which it was originally imbedded, but, as the white-collar crew had gathered to watch me perform, the actor in me took over, and perform I did.

During the next few moments I gave a superlative performance. I was the cool, detached, unperturbed scientist at work. I drew my trusty screw driver from my belt, loosened several of the screws from the plug, then tightened them again, strode confidently to the building, worked my way underneath it at the spot where the cord emerged, wriggled the cord in order to let the onlookers know I was progressing with my mysterious healing work, emerged from underneath the building, again made my way to the J-box, and, with a fervent, inward prayer, plunged the cord into the outlet which I had selected for my do or die test.

Glory be and Hallelujah! That building just lit up like a Christmas tree! Thomas Edison could not have experienced a greater thrill in watching his first incandescent lamp sputter and glow than I did as I watched that blessed, dazzling burst of brilliance light up every nook and cranny of that building. My hunch had been correct. If it hadn't worked, and I had no real reason to believe that it would, I would have disgraced not only myself, but our whole crew of electricians. As it was, the Walter Mitty in me rose to the occasion. The office workers, including several attractive members of the feminine sex, cast admiring glances my ways. When one of them flattered me with, "Boy, you electricians sure know your stuff!", I smiled condescendingly, and muttered nonchalantly, "It's all in a day's work." At that moment, I was no "shoe clerk"—I was an electrician!

Our Pets
1958
(Age 52)

Those friends of the DuVals' who have an antipathy towards the furred and feathered creatures of the world have long since learned to make a wide detour when nearing our home. Conversely, those of our friends who love pets know that a visit to our home is always good for a laugh. Whether their name be Tom, Dick, or Harriet, they can expect, when opening the door to our living room to be greeted with a hearty, "Hi, Joe!" by our talking, laughing, throat-clearing mynah bird, Sinbad. At the same time, from another corner of the room would come the cheery notes of the first few bars of reveille with, perhaps a few choice wolf calls from Tippy, the cockatiel, or a warm, deep-throated trill from Frosty, our white crested canary. Gypsy, our friendly maltoodle (Half maltese terrier, half poodle) would also be on hand, her waggly tail begging for a pat on the head to appease her affectionate nature.

But, let's get back to Sinbad. She has a remarkable personality—I say "she", but really we're not sure whether Sinbad is male or female. Sinbad's a beautiful glossy black bird with a yellow set of wattles. Male birds in general are considered more striking-looking than the female, and Sinbad is really a handsome looking bird. The feathers on the top of his head are parted neatly in the middle, a sure sign that he is a Greater Hill mynah, considered the best talkers of them all. Sinbad has a vocabulary of close to twenty words and phrases; sometimes I feel that I can actually carry on a conversation with him. Of course, he responds by association and hasn't the slightest idea what he's talking about. For instance, I can ask him, "Sinbad, who do you love?", and hearing these words he'll come right back with, "I love Sinbad," in a rather doleful voice. I have learned from experience that he usually follows his "Hi, Joe," with a plaintive "Hi", after a few seconds, so when he greets me with "Hi, Joe", I answer, "Hi, Sinbad" and he responds, "Hi." It sounds just as if we were exchanging greetings. My wife, Roz, had been in the habit of saying, "There you are," whenever she fed him, a saying which he readily picked up. Whenever he hears my son David's name mentioned, he'll call "David" in a clear, high falsetto. Many times Roz and I are in the midst of discussing some subject in his presence, when he'll pipe up with "What?" as though he just couldn't understand what we were talking about. He has a beautifully cultured sounding "Hel-lo" and seems to know just the appropriate time to say "Good-bye" although he has occasionally embarrassed a friend by greeting him with "Good-bye".

Sinbad has a delightfully infectious laugh which sounds exactly like Roz with which he surprises us at unexpected moments. We may be watching a comedy TV show late in the evening. We think Sinbad is fast asleep, but when the audience starts laughing, all of a sudden, from deep beneath her cage covering, come peals of merry laughter which drives us into hysterics. He has also picked up a peculiar half-cough, half clearing of the throat reaction which he uses whenever anyone within earshot coughs or clears his throat.

I once caught a friend of ours leaning over the cage, and in a soft, confidential manner, repeating over and over the phrases, "Would you like a dry martini? Would you like a whiskey sour?" while Sinbad listened attentively. Can you imagine our embarrassment when one of our teetotaler friends comes visiting, only to be greeted with "Would you like a dry martini? Would you like a whiskey sour?" Sinbad is a lot of fun, and unlike most talking birds, loves to perform in front of company.

Our first four-footed pet was Feathers, a black and white shaggy type dog which we acquired soon after we were wed in 1940, and who was with us until she died in 1952. Feathers was a Lhasa Apso, a breed which came originally from Tibet. She was about the size of a small terrier, had hair growing over her eyes, which sort of hid them from view, but was necessary to shield them from the sun.

I remember the first night she was with us, I had prepared a nice comfortable bed for her in the kitchen of our apartment. When bed time came, I placed her on her blankets and told her that was where she was expected to sleep. Evidently she didn't understand, for as soon as I got into bed, I heard the quiet pattering of little feet, and up came Feathers to snuggle down at the foot of our bed. Patiently, I got up, carried her back to the kitchen, deposited her gently on her blankets, and went back to bed. A few minutes later, Feathers was again at the foot of our bed. This process was repeated four or five times, but Feathers finally won out, and from then on, for the next twelve years, Feathers slept curled up cozily at the foot of our bed.

Feathers was a lively dog, full of bounce and dash, and during that first year, since we lived in an apartment without any yard, we would take her for many long walks. There was a small park a few blocks from where we lived where she loved to gambol and run, racing around us in wide circles and sometimes tumbling over and over in sheer exuberance. She never did like a leash, so we would walk her without it after teaching her to stop at each curb and never cross the street until we gave the word. She was very good in this respect, and even though she might be a half block ahead of us, she would stop at each corner, sit and wait for us; then as soon as we saw it was safe and gave her permission, she would scoot across the street as fast as her little legs would carry her.

One day while walking down Hollywood Boulevard, we passed a music store in front of which was a larger than life replica of that well-known phonograph with the dog looking into the horn listening to "his master's voice." Feathers came upon this very large plaster of Paris dog without realizing it, backed off hurriedly, then started barking for all she was worth at this strange creature. It was very amusing.

After we moved to the beach, Feathers delighted in romping and running in the sand, loved to dig in it, and enjoyed beach life most thoroughly. We were a bit fearful as to what her reactions would be to a baby in the house, but she took it in stride, and was wonderful with David while he was a growing tot. Although we early taught David to treat her gently, Feathers never protested when he played roughly with her or pulled her fur.

Gypsy, who has been with us since 1952, is also a black and white, or shall I say grey and white shaggy-type dog. Gypsy looks a lot like Daisy, the movie star of a decade ago, and also like Tippie, the well-known cartoon character. We paid fifty dollars for her and were told that was too much to pay for an unpedigreed dog of mixed lineage, but she has paid off with a million dollars of love and laughter. She is very affectionate, but give her a bone, and Dr. Jekyll at once becomes Mr. Hyde; everybody within ten feet of her becomes her mortal enemy from whom she will defend that bone to her last gasp. Gypsy is a wonderful traveler, loves nothing better than to go for a ride in the car, and has made two trips to St. Louis with us, making new friends wherever she went. We once took her to an obedience training school, and she turned out to be the juvenile delinquent of her class. If she didn't want to walk at heel, she would simply turn over on her back and let herself be dragged along. She seldom paid attention, but was forever casting a furtive eye over her shoulder to look for Roz and me. However, although she did not graduate with honors, she has learned to sit, stay, shake hands, speak, and balance a tidbit on her nose, then, when we give the word, snap it up before it falls to the ground. She is also a very honest dog, not giving to snitching food from the table, even though it is something she loves to eat. She loves apples, and whenever we are eating one she sits in front of us, with such a pleading expression in her eyes, she is always rewarded with at least the core. When I am preparing her evening meal, she sits watching me with her little paws crossed in front of her, at which time I call her Patient Griselda. She's our favorite pet, though Sinbad runs her a close second.

Which brings me to Tippy, our whistling, talking cockatiel. Tippy does very well with the first few bars of reveille, can give out with the wolf call, and has a vocabulary which includes "What's the matter, pretty, pretty, pretty boy?" and "Hello, sweetie." Like her predecessor, Tonto, she really loves Gypsy, and all we have to do to get her to perform, is take her out of her cage, bring her to Gypsy, and she starts right in whistling and talking ardently to her. Although we keep Tippy in a cage most of the time, Tonto had the run of the house. She too loved Gypsy, and any time Gypsy showed any disinclination to eat her meals, we would let Tonto approach her food dish and start pecking at the dog food. Gypsy would then wolf it down quickly, before Tonto could do away with her meal. The day after David left for Principia in

1953, Tonto was following Gypsy around in the back bedroom, when a large ugly tomcat, seeing her opportunity, came right into the room, seized Tonto, and made off with her. I had been shaving in the back bathroom, and hearing Tonto's terrific shrieking, came out just in time to see the cat bounding over the back fence with Tonto in her mouth, That was the last we ever saw of him.

Frosty, the white-crested German roller canary was a Christmas gift to Roz from Ruth Peters, her business manager. Frosty has a lovely soft warm-sounding roll, and can hold a note longer than I can hold my breath.

This brings me to Peachy, our peach-faced lovebird. Peachy, it seems, doesn't care for women. Roz has a terrible time feeding him, as Peachy will go for her whenever she as much as puts her hand in the cage. But David or I can reach in, scratch his head and pet him without the least fear of being pecked or bitten. Peachy now has company since Roz recently captured another lovebird which had been visiting in our back yard for about a year, eating the seed spilled around our parakeet aviary. How this bird managed to survive the winter cold and the spring rains, I'll never know, but Roz left a bedroom window open one day, enticed the bird with some bird seed on the sill, and caught him with a butterfly net. He is a bit wild still, and has been named Speck.

In our kitchen is a large cage which, at first glance, seems empty, but upon closer scrutiny, is found to contain a sleeping ball of fur buried underneath the newspapers lining the bottom of the cage. This turns out to be Honey, our kinkajou. A nocturnal animal, Honey sleeps all day, but is awake and lively most of the night. The kinkajou looks like a small honey-bear, though it is a member of the raccoon family. It has a prehensile tail which it uses to hang onto various objects, and also to sit on, much as a kangaroo. Honey is a cute, cuddly animal with a thick coat of brown fur. He doesn't smell, he doesn't shed, he's never been sick in his life, and has a wonderful sense of humor, loves to play tag and hide and seek, scampering across the room with a peculiar bounding motion. He loves fruit of all kinds, carrot sticks, cottage cheese; I make him a regular salad as his regular meal. He'll get up in the morning just in time to watch us squeeze orange juice, gratefully eat the half orange we offer him, and then go back to bed, curling up inside some torn shirts or old pajamas with which we keep him supplied. These animals, when captured as babies, are tame as kittens, but as they grow older they are said to revert to their wild stage. We've had him about five years now, and he is beginning to show these signs occasionally. I suppose we'll have to be rid of him eventually, but in the meantime, he's really been a lot of fun.

Several years ago Roz started breeding parakeets as a hobby. She now has an aviary containing about twenty wild parakeets of various types with which she experiments to produce violets, yellow-faced blues, clear-wing yellows, rainbows, and others. It all started about six years ago when Roz thought it might be fun to try to hatch one nest of birds. She borrowed a pair of parakeets from friend who was a breeder, but got nowhere. However her second pair produced a clutch of eggs which hatched. It was a great thrill to Roz to see those naked, featherless babies emerge from their eggs. She had promised these birds to various friends, and they were so beautiful, and developed into such loquacious talkers, that she kept right on producing nest after nest, and distributing them among her friends. Soon her birds acquired quite a reputation as Mrs. DuVal's talking parakeets, and strangers started calling her to ask if she had any birds for sale. So, she started selling them at five dollars apiece, which helped pay for the aviary and the expense of breeding and feeding. It's really unbelievable, the vocabulary some of these birds have developed, from "My name is Bobby Smith, and I live at" such and such an address to "I'm master here—I'm the boss!" I wouldn't believe it when one of our friends called to say her bird has a vocabulary of over one-hundred words, so we paid him a visit. It was uncanny to hear that little bundle of fluff chatter away. One of her birds went to a German couple who taught him to speak German, while another went to Andre Muzet, who is teaching him to converse in fluent French.

Hardly a day passes but somebody doesn't call Roz to tell her of the condition of Pretty Boy's droppings, or to order a pound or two of the special mixture which Roz uses so successfully in feeding her birds. It has gotten so the Audubon Society has listed Roz as a bird expert, so when someone calls the Society about some special bird problem, they refer them to "Mrs. DuVal". David, who also has become something of an ornithologist, is quite an expert at identifying birds, and was appointed by the local Audubon Society chapter to head their Christmas bird count, which is quite an honor, and which he conducted with thoroughness and dispatch.

There is a big cage in the back patio which serves as the home for our two pet crows. They use the cage just to sleep in at night, and have the run of the yard during the day. Although neither of them have their wings clipped, they make no effort to fly away. Either they're so stupid they just don't realize they're birds, or they're so smart they know a good thing when they see one. I think it's the latter, for they're well-fed and well-loved, and I have heard that crows are about the most intelligent of all birds. We feed them Purina dog food softened in warm milk or water with bits of fruit and vegetables as special treats. They really thrive on this diet, are in splendid condition with black, glossy coats and beady black eyes. Satan, the elder of the two, was acquired as a baby from a rather mercenary little boy who called Roz all excited one morning to tell her he had found this baby crow which had fallen out of its nest, and we could have him for three dollars. It sounded interesting, so we decided to invest three dollars. I must say we got our money's worth. If there is anything bigger and more bottomless looking than the maw of a hungry baby crow, I've never seen it. Satan used to wake us up in the morning with her hungry cawing which would continue until she was satiated. We would stuff dog food into her wide-open mouth, and she would sound something like, "CAW! CAW! gulp, gulp—CAW! CAW! gulp, gulp," and so on until her stomach was filled. Both birds love their baths, and it's really a delight to watch them splash around in a large dishpan full of water which we keep in the yard expressly for their use. Satan loves to have her head scratched and will stand with wings outspread and head lowered, emitting long, contented "ooooo"s as we scratch the top of her head. The crows get along fine together, but woe betide any pigeon that might come in for a stray meal—they'll attack en masse and drive him out.

Perhaps the easiest pet of all to care for is the desert tortoise. We have three, all of which are happily oblivious to their surroundings, hibernating under some pile of debris in a dark corner of the garage. They spend half the year in hibernation, emerging sometimes in late March or early April. They feed on weeds and grass, supplemented by lettuce leaves. They require hardly any water, and in autumn, gorge themselves on figs which have fallen from our usually quite productive fig tree. Originally we had two tortoises, James and Janet, although we eventually learned that James should have been named Janet and vice versa. Each year James would lay a clutch of eggs, and each year we did our best to get them to hatch, but with no success. Eventually, we hope to be able to carry this project through to a successful conclusion, and then won't we have fun, with a bunch of baby tortoises running loose in our yard.

It's only one step from tortoises to turtles, of which we also have our share. These are David's hobby, and he has quite a collection. This consists of a dozen specimens covering nine different species. Of the five types of box turtle in the United States, he has three. He's sunk an old kitchen sink into some ground next to the house, which he keeps filled with water. These water turtles go into hibernation also during the winter, burrowing deep in the mud surrounding the basin.

During the course of our married life we have at one time or another had about every type of pet one can imagine. Rabbits, ducks, hamsters, baby alligators, even a snake which Roz and Paquita found in the highway while motoring one day. This snake, a king snake, was about the most uninteresting pet we ever had. He just lay there, torpid, refused to eat, and after a few days, we took him out to the adjoining farmland and released him.

During the days when we still had Feathers, before our home became a haven for a houseful of birds, we somehow became the owners of a black cat which we promptly named Tar. So we then had Tar and Feathers. Tar and Feathers soon became fast friends, and it was a delight to watch them wrestle, rolling over and over, simulating fierceness, but never hurting each other. Feathers would tolerate no other cats on the premises, and Tar would keep our yard free of stray dogs, but the two of them were inseparable.

During the war we had a half dozen white Leghorn chickens, which really couldn't be classified as pets, but which furnished us with the most delicious fresh eggs I ever tasted.

Some years ago we were visited each spring by a pair of blue jays which stayed with us throughout the summer, raised their family, then left for parts unknown. We called them Jimmy and Jenny, and they became so tame that David would feed them peanuts which they took right out of his hand. One spring they made their nest in the lower branches of our fig tree. One day Roz noticed that one of the babies had fallen to the ground. She picked it up and gently placed it back in the nest. Instead of swooping down to attack her as she half expected, the parent birds chattered their thanks and actually seemed appreciative. This happened several times. One morning while we were still in bed, we heard an excited chattering outside our bedroom accompanied by a terrific rapping on the window pane of the glass door of the bedroom. Jimmy and Jenny were doing their best to get our attention. Roz opened the door, looked out, and, sure enough, there was that baby jay on the grass. She picked it up and replaced it in the nest while the parent jays hopped around, again jabbering their thanks. I've heard it said that wild birds will not go near their young after they have been touched by human hands, but this incident proved that this is not always the case. A remarkable instance of intelligence demonstrated by one of the most intelligent of birds, the blue jay.

Roz once came home from a meeting of the Aviculture Society with a door prize. The Aviculture Society, by the way, is composed of a group of bird breeders. Her prize was alive, and looked at first glance like a bundle of white feathers. It was hard for me to tell which was the head and which the tail, for this was a Silky bantam rooster almost entirely covered with thick white feathers, even down to his claws. Eb, as Roz fondly called him, was a good pet in many ways. He was companionable. and would follow Roz around like a little puppy, scratching for worms in the soil beside her, as Roz dug in the garden. He had one liability, however—He would welcome the sun's rising in characteristic rooster fashion, and as we were in close proximity to our neighbors, this would never do. We tried taking him in each night and placing him under a box in the bathroom. This didn't work our too satisfactorily, and eventually we were forced to give him away—for the sake of peace in the community.

Another pet which didn't last too long because he threatened to disrupt the good neighbor policy, was Touky, a beautiful, brilliantly colored toucan, that strange looking bird with the elongated bill that made him look like his name should be "Schnozzle." He was an interesting character, and it was fun to watch him pick up a grape with the tip of his beak, then let it roll down his foot-long bill to his gullet. We had to get rid of him, though. He had a raucous voice which sounded for all the world like the ripping of a piece of old, dry canvas, and that had a carrying power that could be heard throughout the entire neighborhood. We sold him eventually to a bird breeding friend of ours who had a female toucan. The last we heard they had happily set up housekeeping, and our friend promised us a baby toucan out of the first nest that hatched. Can you imagine anything as cute as a baby toucan? We can hardly wait.

That's about all I can think of about the pets around our home. Some people think we're not quite normal. Maybe they're right. Anyhow, as we used to say in radio, "You don't have to be crazy, but it helps!"

VOLKOVITSKY TIME-LINE

THREADS

There are two types of historical threads that weave back and forth from the past to the future, constantly affecting the present. One type is that which we see surviving disease and war, pogrom and holocaust, accident and chance, which leads from one individual to the next until it arrives at *you*. If any of these events had prevented the birth of children, you would not have been born. The decisions made by one's ancestors during their lifetimes are a vital part of the foundation of your existence. This is truly incredible considering how many direct ancestors you have after only a few generations.

Another thread is one that weaves a path for the future. We're not aware of it; often we cannot do anything about it. It normally is not something our decisions or those of our ancestors can affect. It is a preparation for the future—events which must occur in order for future decisions to be made.

Both of these threads can be seen in the fabric of our family history. For example, eventually our family will move to the New World. Many things must happen first before this can occur, and one of those events happens now. 1492 marks the landing of Columbus. Perhaps he wasn't the first. But this event is symbolic of the discovery of what was to be called America. And it is the first vision of that thread which would eventually lead to our being here.

The Time-Line is an attempt at placing our family history against the backdrop of what was happening in the world at that time. Much was happening at these times, but I have tried to list not only what was important at the time but what also was happening that might have affected them either at that time or in the future.

TIME-LINE

The Time-Line goes from the earliest evidence of Jews in Ukraine in the sixth century to the Naturalization of Peysach in the twentieth century.

The events that are memorable in Borzna are framed and printed in italics. Other events memorable to the Volkovitsky and Sovitsky families are also framed but not printed in italics.

Events in Russia/Ukraine history are given in the first column.
Events in American history are given in the second column.
Events in European history are given in the third column.

Placing one's self in the point in time in which various events were happening gives a sense of *being there*. Seeing where one's family was or might have been makes the history come alive. It gives a base for wondering about the WHY.

As one writer puts it, "History *is* biography."[66] This same person writes, "When you study the lives of individuals, you must also study history…You cannot separate people from the context of their times, because the steel of inner character is hammered out on the anvil of time, and forged in the context of history."[67] We're not looking at events. We're looking at people's lives. Ralph Waldo Emerson wrote, "There is properly no history; only biography." Our family's "biography" takes place within the "biographies" of others, influencing it to a greater or lesser extent.

CALENDARS

Before proceeding further, an understanding of calendars needs to be established. A great deal is made here of dates, whether in a time line or within personal memoirs. It is important to place occurrences and peoples within periods of history and to relate these to one's own history to make these vital and alive.

---

[66] Charles R. Swindoll, *Moses*, p.191.
[67] Charles R. Swindoll, *Elijah*, p.3.

Calendars are themselves artificial measurements of time which itself is a man-made dimension. Considering this, although a timeline is interesting, it must be taken with a grain of salt.

There have been numerous attempts to measure calendar time. Hebrew, Chinese and Islamic calendars are but three early types. The ones that are most important to us are the Julian and Gregorian calendars, and the problem here is that the year is actually not exactly 365 days. Therefore, a leap year was added to periodically make provision for this.

During the first century a solar year was accepted to be 365.25 days. Julius Caesar accepted this and directed that this calendar be put into use. (Within this "Julian" calendar, the month Quintilis became July after Julius and Sextilis became August after Augustus.)

In 1582 it was obvious that the Julian Calendar needed reform. The year was too long and became increasingly out of phase with the seasons. By 1545 the vernal equinox, which determined Easter, had moved 10 days from its proper date. Therefore, by dropping seven years and establishing a revised system of Leap Years Pope Gregory XIII instituted the Gregorian Calendar. The Julian Calendar became known as "OLD STYLE"; the Gregorian Calendar as "NEW STYLE".

Like this country's Daylight Saving Time, there were some areas that accepted the Gregorian reform and others which didn't. Most European countries adopted it. England and its colonies held out until 1752. France waited for Napoleon to institute it on 1806.

The dates within this document are particularly confusing, because Russia didn't convert until after the Revolution in 1918. In between, an Eternal Calendar was introduced in 1929 (with 30-day months.) But the Gregorian was readopted in 1940! Even today the Eastern Orthodox Church still uses a version of the Julian Calendar (which explains why their celebrations of Christmas and Easter are different from those of other Christian churches.)

I don't know whether the Julian or Gregorian calendars were used for the birth and other historical dates. Most of the Volkoff dates are prior to 1918. I surmise that those dates for events within Ukraine are Old Style dates. Usually anyone born in Russia prior to 1918 was born under the Julian Calendar. Those dates which came from American ship arrivals or for events occurring in America would be New Style dates.

VOLKOVITSKY TIME-LINE

587 B.C.—Nebuchadnezzar deports Jews to Caucasus.
970—Jews flee north to Kiev.
987—Jews attempt to convert Prince Vladimir to Judaism.
988—Vladimir adopts Christianity in Kievan Rus
2nd Century—Jews in Crimea
          Jews occupy own quarter in Kiev ("Zhidy")
1056-1114—Nestor (Russian Chronicles)

1066-William conquers Normandy
1095-1229-Crusades
1100-Arabic numerals in Europe
1215-Magna Carta
1162-1227-Genghis Khan unites Mongols
1350-1400-Age of Chaucer
1337-1453 100 Years War
1348-'50 "Black Death"
1431-Joan of Arc executed
1475-Rifle invented
1492-Columbus sights land (10/12)
1452-1519 Leonardo do Vinci
1517-Luther's 95 Theses
1519-Aztec Empire, Cortez takes Mexico
1543-Copernicus
1564-1616 Age of Shakespeare
1564-1642 Galileo

1648 Ukrainian peasants led by Bogdan Chmielnicki kill 200,000 Jews in Eastern regions
In ten years seven hundred Jewish communities wiped out.

> **1633 *Borzna founded***

1654-1667 Poland/Lithuania war with Ukrainian Cossacks—lose much territory.

1654-First Jews arrive in New Amsterdam   1664 Moliere's *Tartuffe*

1682-1725 Reign of Peter the First.
1683-William Penn signs treaty with Delaware
Indians for Pennsylvania   1687-Newton's The Principia

1703 St. Petersburg founded
1727 Catherine I expels Jews from Russia.
1739 All Jews ordered to leave territory annexed by Russia from Ukraine (A century of Ambivalence—p.XIV).
1772-1795 Poland succumbs to three successive partitions by Russia, Prussia and Austria.

> **1782 *Borzna becomes county town in Chernihiv gubernia***

AMERICAN REVOLUTION
1773-Boston Tea Party
1774-First Continental Congress
1776-Declaration of Independence
1787-Constitution adopted
1788-George Washington chosen president
1791-Bill of Rights adopted

Industrial Revolution in England
1792-French Revolution

<u>1794</u> Catherine II issues ukase establishing Pale of Settlement.
<u>1795</u> 3rd Partition of Poland—Poland not on map.
<u>1801</u> Alexander I.

1803-Napolean sold Louisiana (to Canadian border) to U.S.A.
1804-Lewis and Clark expedition
Aaron Burr shoots Alexander Hamilton
1807-Fulton invents steamboat
1812-War of 1812 begins
1814-F. S. Key writes *Star Spangled Banner*
1819-First part-steam, part-sail-powered crossing of Atlantic, Georgia to Liverpool (29days)
1823-Monroe Doctrine

1804-Napolean declares himself Emperor
1812-15 Grimm's *Fairy Tales*
1815-Napolean defeated at Waterloo

<u>1825</u> Reign of Nicholas I begins
Reign marked by oppression and attempts at conversion to Christianity (Decembrist uprising.)

1825-First steam locomotive in U.S.

Age of Rousseau, Goethe, Beethoven, Poe, Glinka

<u>1827</u> <u>(Aug)</u> Military conscription and school decrees
<u>1827-1854</u> 70,000 Russian Jews conscripted (50,000 minors)

1828-First Webster Dictionary

1831-Nat Turner leads slave rebellion
1836-Texans besieged in Alamo

1832-1884 Reform bills extend rights to Jews & others
1833 Slavery barred in British Empire
1837-Photography (Daguerre)

1840's-'50's Generation of Moishe Nosavitsky/Feigel

1841-First emigrant wagon train leaves for California from Missouri (6 months)
1842-First use of anesthetic
Oregon Trail begins
1844-First telegraph message
1845-Texas admitted to Union (12/29)
1846-Mexican War begins
Elias Howe invents sewing machine
1847-First adhesive postage stamp
Emerson/Longfellow publish

<u>1848</u> *Communist Manifesto*—Marx
    1848-Gold discovered in California
    1851-*Moby Dick*
    1852-*Uncle Tom's Cabin*
    1853-Japan opened to U.S. shipping
      Republican Party formed
      Thoreau's *Walden*

<u>1855</u> Nicholas I dies—Reign of Alexander II begins
    1855-Whitman's *Leaves of Grass*
    1857-Dred Scott decision
    1858-First Atlantic cable
    1859-Harpers Ferry   1859 Darwin's *The Origin if Species*

**1860's-'70's Generation of parents of Peysach and Motley
(Israel Baruch & Arya Leib)**

Napolean III with British and Turks declares war on Russia. Crimean defeat causes Czar Alexander II to begin series of progressive reforms.

<u>1861</u>-Emancipation of serfs
    1861-Abraham Lincoln elected
    1861-1865 American Civil War

<u>1864</u>-Russian Judiciary reforms military service reduced from 25 years to 6 years
<u>1867</u>-Russia sells Alaska
   Kingdom of Poland abolished; becomes Russian province
     First Kentucky Derby
     1876-Custer's "last stand"
      Twain publishes *Tom Sawyer*
      Hayes declared president

1878—PeysachVolkovitsky born in Borzna (August 8)

   1879-First Woolworth five-and-ten store   1880-Massive immigration from Europe to
                     U.S. begin
   1880-Garfield elected president

Pogrom in Borzna begins August 6, 1880

1880—Motley Sovitsky born in Borzna (September)

1881-Pres. Garfield shot
1883-Brooklyn Bridge opened
1881 Alexander II assassinated—3/1   1884-Cleveland elected president
Geronimo surrenders (9/4)
American Federation of Labor formed by
25 craft unions (Dec 8)
1888-Harrison declared president by Electoral
College
1891 "Talk of America" (see Howe, p.27)
1892 "Nutcracker" (Tchaikovsky)
1894 Nicholas II begins reign

1895—Itska Nosovitsky selling spirits in Borzna

1897—*Borzna population 12,000*

1899—Peysach Volkovitsky marries Motley Sovitsky in Borzna (August)

1897-1899 Anti-Jewish riots

1901—Sarah Volkovitsky born in Borzna (July 4)

1902—Rebecca Volkovitsky born in Borzna (September 26)

1903—Jews expelled from Kiev Pogroms in Kishinef and Homel
1904—Russo-Japanese War begins February—30,000 Jews sent to Far East.
Kishinev Massacre

1905—First Hershey Chocolate Bar

1904—Florence Volkovitsky born in Borzna (March 8)
Peysach to New York, July 18—becomes Peter Volkoff.
Intention to become American citizen filed November 26.

1905—**Peysach** moves to La Crosse, Wisconsin (March)
Motley Volkovitsky to New York (May 29) (with children: Sarah, Bekie, Florence—**becomes** Martha Volkoff

1906—**Joseph Volkoff** born in La Crosse, Wisconsin (August 8)

1908—**Rosy Volkoff** born in La Crosse, Wisconsin (March 18)

1910—**Bertha Volkoff** born in La Crosse, Wisconsin (May 19)

1917—**Peysach** becomes American citizen (May 12), includes Motley, Sara, Rebecca, and Florence

BIBLIOGRAPHY

1. Benet, Michael, <u>RE: Searched ancient document and found ancestor</u>, e-mail, New York, 26 May 1999.

2. Charnofsky, Michael, *Jewish Life in the Ukraine; A Family Saga*, Exposition Press, New York, 1965.

3. Chijner, M. P., *To Kiev by horsedrawn sled, e-mail* 28 Feb 2000.

4. Comey, Joan, *The Diaspora Story: The Epic of the Jewish People Among the Nations,* Random House, New York, 1981.

5. Davidson, Marshall B., *Life in America*, Vol. II, Houghton Mifflin Company, Boston, 1951

6. Dunne, Thomas, *Ellis Island*, W.W. Norton and Company Inc., New York, 1971.

7. Eliach, Yaffa, *There Once was a World; A 900 Year Chronicle of the Shtetl of Eishyshok*, Little Brown, New York, NY, 1998.

8. Fluek, Toby Knobel, *Memories of My Life in a Polish Village, 1930-1949*, Alfref A. Knopf (Random House), New York, 1990.

9. Frey, David, e-mail, Victoria, Australia, 8 May 1999.

10. Gilbert, Martin, *The Jewish Atlas*, Macmillan

11. Goldman, David, <u>Leaving Family Behind in Russia</u>, e-mail, 7 May 1999.

12. Goldstein, Louise, <u>Leaving Family Behind in Russia</u>, e-mail, 8 May 1999

13. Gray, Bettyanne, *Manyas's Story: Faith and Survival in Revolutionary Russia*, Runestone Press, Minneapolis, 1995.

14. Guber, Rafi, <u>Re: Ellis Island: It might help to know why the myth is a myth</u>, e-mail, 21 Jun 1999.

15. Guzik, Estell, <u>19th Conference on Jewish Genealogy, Aug 8-13, 1999-Khazars & Europe Map</u>, e-mail, 20 Apr 1999.

16. Howe, Irving and Kenneth Libo, *World of Our Fathers*, Harcourt Brace Jovanovich, New York and London, 1976.

17. Jonas, Susan, *Ellis Island, Echoes from a Nation's Past*, National Park Service, U.S.. Department of the Interior.

18. Kubijovyc, Volodymyr [Editor], *Encyclopedia of Ukraine*, 5 v., University of Toronto Press, Toronto; Buffalo, 1984.

19. LaFranchi, Howard, *It took a village to save their children*, The Christian Science Monitor, p1, Monday, October 30, 2000.

20. Maimouni, Miriam, <u>RE: Found ancestor in ancient document</u>, e-mail, Berlin, Germany.

21. Margolis, Bernard, <u>The cost of a transatlantic cruise in 1905</u>, e-mail, 26 Feb 2002.

22. Murphy, Dean E., *Jews Remember Horrors of Auschwitz; Poland: Hundreds meet on eve of liberation's anniversary. Their solemn gathering precedes official ceremonies*, Los Angeles Times—PART A, Friday, January 27, 1995.

23. Nearenberg, Mark, e-mail, New York.

24. Paley, Grace, *Enormous Changes at the Last Minute; Stories*, Farrar, Straus, Giroux,New York, 1974.

25. Pickens, Israel, <u>Why do we do all this</u>, e-mail, 1 Aug 1999.

26. Raizman, Marc, Re: <u>the Name Changes</u>, e-mail, 19 Jun 1999

27. Remnick, David, *Lenin's Tomb*, Random House, New York, 1993.

28. Rivers, Dorothy Auerbach, The Courage of our Ancestors, e-mail, 23 Jan 2001.

29. Roskies, Diane K., and David G. Roskies [compiled by], *The Shtetl Book*, Ktav Publishing House, New York, 1975.

30. Shainberg, Maurice, *Breaking from the KGB*, Steimatske Publishing of North America, New York, NY, 1986.

31. Sholom Aleichem, *Sholom Aleichem: Some Laughter, Some Tears*, G.P.Putnam's Sons, New York, 1968.

32. Smith, Eugene, *Passenger Ships of the World, Past and Present*, C.H.Dean, Boston, Massachusetts, 1978.

33. Showel, Charlotte A., Tracing an Old Tune, e-mail, Las Vegas, Nevada, 28 May 1999.

34. Swindoll, Charles R., *Moses*, Word Publishing, Nashville, Tennessee, 1999.

35. ———, *Elijah*, Word Publishing, Nashville, Tennessee, 2000.

36. Tappan, Eva March, ed., *The World's Story: A History of the World in Story, Song and Art*, Vol. VI: Russia, Austria-Hungary,The Balkan States, and Turkey, Boston: Houghton Mifflin, 1914

37. Tift, William S., *Ellis Island*, W.W. Norton & Company Inc., New York, 1971.

38. Volk, Shelley, Leaving Family Behind in Russia, e-mail, Chicago, Illinois, 7 May 1999.

39. Waife-Goldberg, Marie, *My Father; Sholom Aleichem*, Simon and Schuster, New York,1968.

40. Wall, Jay D., Borzna, e-mail, 20 Jul 2000.

41. Wegner, Judith Romney, Info on Pogroms, e-mail, 12 November 2000.

42. Werbach, Mel, <u>A nonsense rhyme: within the family, the shtetl or?</u>, e-mail, Tarzana, California, 30 May 1999.

43. <u>www.friends-partners.org/partners/beyond-the-pale/english/31.html</u>, Beyond the Pale—The History of Jews in Russia.

44. <u>www.us-isreal.org/jsource/History/pale.html</u>, The Pale of Settlement.

0-595-31967-X

12988922R00123

Made in the USA
Lexington, KY
08 January 2012